# Retire Riches

The Master Key to Achieve Financial Freedom & stress-free Retirement.

ANURAG MISHRA
AUTHOR

**BLUEROSE PUBLISHERS**
India | U.K.

Copyright © Anurag Mishra 2025

All rights reserved by author. No part of this publication may be reproduced, stored in a retrieval system or transmitted in any form or by any means, electronic, mechanical, photocopying, recording or otherwise, without the prior permission of the author. Although every precaution has been taken to verify the accuracy of the information contained herein, the publisher assumes no responsibility for any errors or omissions. No liability is assumed for damages that may result from the use of information contained within.

Blue Rose Publishers takes no responsibility for any damages, losses, or liabilities that may arise from the use or misuse of the information, products, or services provided in this publication.

For permissions requests or inquiries regarding this publication, please contact:

BLUEROSE PUBLISHERS
www.BlueRoseONE.com
info@bluerosepublishers.com
+91 8882 898 898
+4407342408967

ISBN: 978-93-7018-047-5

Cover Design: Neeraj kumar sharma
Typesetting: Sagar

First Edition: April 2025

*"Om Namah Shivaya*

*The Universe bows to Lord Shiva*

*I Bow to Lord Shiva"*

*"Nam Myoho Renge Kyo"*

### *Blessing of Kul Devi Nari Samri*

*"May Kul Devi Nari Samri bestow her divine blessings upon this book, **Retire Riches**. May it serve as a guiding light for all who seek financial wisdom and abundance. With her grace, may the knowledge within these pages empower individuals to achieve prosperity, security, and a life of dignity. May obstacles be removed, opportunities be revealed, and success flow effortlessly to those who embrace this wisdom. Let this book inspire generations to build wealth with righteousness and share their success with others. Under her divine protection, may all readers walk the path of financial freedom with confidence and peace. Jai Maa Nari Samri!"*

*"Retirement is not the end of earning; it's the test of how well you planned while you were earning."- Anurag*

# Preface

Retirement is not just about stopping work; it's about achieving financial freedom, security, and the ability to live life on your own terms. In a world where financial uncertainty looms large, preparing for a stress-free retirement is not just a luxury—it's a necessity.

***Retire Riches*** is more than just a book; it's a roadmap to financial independence. Whether you are in your 20s, 30s, 40s, 50s or even nearing retirement, this book will provide you with the knowledge, strategies, and insights needed to build, grow, and protect your wealth.

***"Do not save what is left after spending, but spend what is left after saving." – Warren Buffett***

Through real-life examples, proven investment techniques, and step-by-step financial planning, this book simplifies complex financial concepts into actionable steps. It covers everything from savings and investments to passive income generation and tax-efficient strategies tailored specifically for the Indian audience.

As someone who has spent years guiding individuals toward financial independence, I have seen firsthand how the right knowledge can transform lives. This book is a culmination of years of research, experience, and lessons learned. My mission is to empower you with financial literacy so you can create a future where money works for you, not the other way around.

*"Financial freedom is available to those who learn about it and work for it." – Robert Kiyosaki*

I encourage you to read this book with an open mind and a willingness to take action. The journey to financial freedom starts with a single step, and *Retire Riches* will be your companion in that journey.

Here's to a secure, abundant, and fulfilling retirement!

*Anurag Mishra*
Author & Founder, *Retire Riches Club*

# *Before You start Reading this book Further, Ask Yourself These Hard Questions?*

### 1. Facing an Uncertain Future

👉 *What if, at 60, you still had to work just to pay your bills— without any choice to retire?*

### 2. Depending on Others

👉 *Would you be comfortable depending on your children or relatives for financial support when you're old?*

### 3. Rising Costs & Medical Emergencies

👉 *What if a sudden medical emergency drained all your savings— how would you survive the rest of your life?*

### 4. Dreams vs. Reality

👉 *You've worked hard your whole life. Do you want to spend your golden years enjoying life, or worrying about money?*

### 5. Inflation & Regret

👉 *What if you realize at 55 that your savings aren't enough—when it's too late to fix it?*

### 6. The Harsh Truth

👉 *If you don't start planning today, will you have the right to complain about your financial struggles later?*

### 7. A Simple Question

👉 *Are you ready to sacrifice your peace of mind just because you didn't take action when you had the chance?*

Retirement planning is **not an option**—*it's a necessity. The best time to start was yesterday. The second-best time is NOW.*

*If your answer is "No," then read this book thoroughly to achieve a stress-free retirement.*

**Right now, you have two choices:**

✘ **Ignore retirement planning and struggle later** - facing financial insecurity, dependence, and regret.

✅ **Take action today and build wealth** - ensuring freedom, dignity, and a fulfilling retirement.

This book is your roadmap to **financial security and peace of mind.** Every chapter is designed to help you:

◈ Understand the power of **compounding** and smart investing.

◈ Create a **realistic and achievable retirement plan.**

◈ Learn **where, when, and how to invest** for maximum growth.

◈ Avoid **common mistakes** that destroy wealth.

◈ Ensure **you never have to depend on anyone financially.**

**The earlier you start, the easier your journey will be.** Read this book with focus, apply what you learn, and take control of your future.

◈ **Your retirement should be a time of freedom—not financial stress.** Let's make it happen!

***Retire Riches***

*The Master Key to Achieve Financial Freedom
& stress-free Retirement.*

# Contents

Chapter 1: Introduction to Retirement Planning ........................... 4

Chapter 2: Understanding Your Retirement Needs .................... 16

Chapter 3: Retirement Goals and Setting Milestones ............... 23

Chapter 4: Investment Strategies for Retirement ....................... 30

Chapter 5: Tax Planning for Retirement ...................................... 38

Chapter 6: Creating a Retirement Budget ................................... 46

Chapter 7: Managing Post-Retirement Income .......................... 54

Chapter 8: Retirement Planning for Specific Goals ................... 63

Chapter 9: Retirement Planning for Small Business Owners .... 71

Chapter 10: Retirement Planning for Women's ......................... 79

Chapter 11: Retirement Planning for Senior Citizens ................ 87

Chapter 12: Retirement Planning for Couples ........................... 95

Chapter 13: Retirement Planning for Self-Employed Individuals & Entrepreneur's. .................................................... 104

Chapter 14: Retirement Planning for High Net-Worth Individuals (HNWI) .................................................................... 113

Chapter 15: Retirement Planning for Different Stages of Life ............................................................................... 123

Chapter16: Real Estate Mis selling in India ............................. 131

Chapter 17: Awareness Regarding Financial
Scams in India..............................................................................137

Chapter 18: Insurance Mis-Selling in India ...............................145

Chapter 19: The Role of a Financial Advisor
in Retirement Planning................................................................151

Chapter 20: Challenges in Retirement Planning .......................155

Chapter 21: The Importance of Estate Planning &
Legacy Building in Retirement Planning...................................161

Chapter 22: Conclusion and Action Plan for
Retirement Planning....................................................................169

# Special Thanks

I would like to take this moment to express my deepest gratitude to the incredible people who have supported me throughout this journey. This book would not have been possible without the love, encouragement, and strength of my Guru, my family, friends, and mentors.

"With deep reverence and gratitude, we extend our heartfelt thanks to **Premanand Ji Maharaj** for his divine wisdom, guidance, and blessings. His teachings continue to inspire and illuminate our paths, filling our lives with peace, devotion, and righteousness. May his grace always be with us."

A heartfelt thank you to my Mentors—***Bharat Bansal, Barun Mishra, Gaurav, Munna Lal Ji, and Jitender Chaudhary***. Your invaluable guidance, wisdom, and insights have shaped my thoughts and actions throughout this process. Your mentorship has played a crucial role in bringing this vision to life, and for that, I am truly grateful.

To my wonderful parents, ***Karuna and Shyam Bihari Mishra,*** your endless love, wisdom, and unwavering belief in me have been my greatest source of strength. To my elder brothers, ***Kartikay*** and ***Kunal,*** your constant support and motivation have always been a guiding light. I am also deeply grateful to my Bhabhi, ***Shruti***, and my beautiful nieces, ***Avigna and Anaya***, for being such a cherished part of my life.

To my amazing wife, ***Monika Mishra***—your love, patience, and understanding have been my backbone. You have stood by me through every step of this journey, and for that, I am truly grateful. To my beloved daughters, *Miraya and Amyra,* you inspire me every day with your laughter and boundless energy, reminding me why I strive to create a bright future.

To my in-laws—*Mummy, Papa, Sonia, Amit Ji, Shiv, Lovely, Himanshu,* and our ever-joyful companions, *Chester* and *Boo Boo*—your kindness and encouragement have been a blessing. Thank you for believing in me and always having my back.

A heartfelt thanks to all my maternal relatives for their endless love and support and to my paternal relatives for their constant encouragement. Your influence and care have shaped me in ways words cannot fully express.

A special thank you to my team members—*Niranjan, Sandeep, Praveen, and Kapil*. Your dedication, hard work, and unwavering support have been instrumental in this journey. I truly appreciate your contributions and commitment.

I am forever grateful to each of you. Your love and support have been the foundation upon which this book was built, making this journey all the more meaningful.

With heartfelt thanks,
*Author Anurag Mishra*

*Retire Riches*

***"The question isn't at what age I want to retire; it's at what income."*** *– George Foreman*

## Chapter 1:
# Introduction to Retirement Planning

**The Importance of Retirement Planning in India**

In India, retirement planning is an often-neglected aspect of financial planning. Many individuals assume that they will be able to rely on their children or government pension schemes after retirement. However, with the changing economic landscape and increasing life expectancy, this assumption can be a risky one. By starting early and planning systematically, individuals can ensure a financially secure retirement.

**Key Challenges for Indian Retirees**

- **Inflation:** The cost of living in India is rising rapidly, and inflation has a direct impact on the purchasing power of your savings.

- **Healthcare Costs:** With age comes increased health-related expenses, and healthcare in India can be expensive, especially for those without adequate insurance coverage.

- **Dependence on Family:** Many people in India rely on their children for post-retirement support, which may not always be a sustainable solution.

*Common Misconceptions About Retirement Planning in India*

- ➤ **Misconception 1: "I can depend on the government pension."** The reality is that not all Indians have access to government pension schemes. The **Employees' Provident Fund (EPF)** and **Public Provident Fund (PPF)** are great, but their contributions may not be sufficient to meet all your retirement needs. In fact, the government's pension schemes are often designed only for employees in the formal sector.

- ➤ **Misconception 2: "I can always work even after retirement."** While many individuals may continue working after retirement, it's not guaranteed. Depending on physical and mental health, one may not be able to work for an income later in life.

- ➤ **Misconception 3: "Retirement is far away; I have plenty of time."** This is the most dangerous myth. Retirement may seem distant, but the sooner you begin planning and saving, the better equipped you'll be to handle unforeseen expenses or emergencies. Time, combined with consistent investing, is your biggest ally.

- ➤ **Misconception 4: My Children Will Take Care of me."** While traditionally, children were expected to support parents, changing lifestyles, nuclear families, and increasing life expectancy mean that financial independence is crucial.

- ➤ **Misconception 5: Investing in Fixed Deposits (FDs) Is the Best Strategy''** While FDs are safe, they may not provide returns that beat inflation. Diversifying with mutual funds, PMS stocks, or

National Pension System (NPS) can help generate better post-retirement income.

- ➢ **Misconception 6: Real Estate Is the Best Retirement Investment"** Though real estate is a valuable asset, it may not always provide liquidity when needed. A well-balanced portfolio with Mutual funds, stocks, and pension plans* is always advisable.

- ➢ **Misconception 7: I Can Start Saving After Major Expenses Are Covered''** Delaying retirement savings for children's education, home loans, or other expenses can reduce financial security. A balance between present needs and future goals is essential.

## *Conclusion*

A well-planned retirement strategy involves early savings, diverse investments, inflation adjustments, and contingency planning. Avoiding these misconceptions can help ensure financial security in the golden years.

## *The Power of Compounding & Early Investing Pay off – Your Key to Wealth Creation*

### *Introduction*

***Albert Einstein*** once called compounding the "eighth wonder of the world." Why? Because it has the potential to turn even small savings into a massive fortune over time.

Compounding is the process where your investments generate earnings, and those earnings, in turn, generate more earnings. The longer your money stays invested, the more exponential the growth.

Imagine a snowball rolling down a hill—it starts small, but as it moves, it collects more snow and grows bigger. That's exactly how compounding works in the world of finance.

### *The Indian Bamboo Tree: A Story of Patience, Persistence, and the Power of Compounding*

### *The Story:*

In a small village in India, a young man named ***Vansh*** dreamed of financial success. He envied businessmen who made quick money in the stock market and wanted to achieve the same wealth overnight.

One evening, he sat beside his Dadaji (grandfather), a wise elder known for his experience in life and money. "Dadaji, how can I become rich quickly?" he asked.

Dadaji smiled and handed him a handful of Indian bamboo seeds. "Plant these, water them daily, and I'll share the secret to wealth."

Eager to learn, ***Vansh*** planted the seeds and watered them every day.

A month passed. Nothing happened.

Six months passed. Still, nothing.

A year passed. Then two, then three—yet not a single sprout appeared above the soil.

Frustrated, **Vansh's** friend **Amit** laughed at him. "You're wasting time! Look at me—I made a fortune trading stocks and crypto. Why wait for something that isn't growing?"

Doubt crept into **Vansh's** mind. Maybe **Amit** was right. Maybe this was pointless.

But each time he thought of giving up, he remembered his grandfather's words:
***"Patience, persistence, and faith."***

So, he continued watering the seeds.

Then, in the fifth year, something unbelievable happened. The bamboo sprouted—and within a few weeks, it grew over 80 feet!

Shocked, **Vansh** ran to Dadaji. "How did this happen? It did nothing for years, and now it's growing like magic!"

Dadaji chuckled. "For five years, the bamboo was growing its roots underground—building a strong foundation. Only when it was ready did it grow at an unstoppable pace."

**The Lesson: Compounding is Like the Indian Bamboo Tree**

At that moment, **Vansh** understood the secret of true wealth—it follows the same principle as compounding investments.

> ➢ Early Investments (The Seed Phase): Your savings may seem small, like seeds in the soil. Growth is invisible at first.

- Years of Patience (The Root Phase): Your investments are strengthening beneath the surface. Though progress seems slow, wealth is being built.

- The Breakthrough (The Growth Phase): After years of discipline, your wealth multiplies at an astonishing pace, much like the bamboo shooting up after years of waiting.

***The biggest mistake? Digging up the seeds too soon—just like withdrawing investments early.***

*Vansh* finally realized why successful investors stay patient. He started investing in mutual funds through SIPs, avoiding the lure of quick-money Ponzi schemes. Over time, his disciplined approach helped his small investments blossom into a fortune—proving that time and consistency are the real keys to financial success.

**Final Thought:**

***Wealth, like the Indian bamboo tree, takes time to grow. But when it does, the rewards are beyond imagination.***

**Understanding the Power of Compounding**

To illustrate, let's take a simple example:

**Example 1:** *Amit V/s. Himanshu* **– The Early Investor Wins**

Let's compare two friends, **Amit and Himanshu**, who both want to build wealth.

- **Amit** starts investing ₹5,000 per month at age 25 and stops at 45 (20 years of investing).

- **Himanshu** delays his investment and starts at 40, investing ₹10,000 per month until 60 (20 years of investing).

Both invest for 20 years, but **Amit** starts earlier.

Final Corpus at Age 60 (Assuming 12% Annual Returns)

- ➢ **Amit's** Corpus (₹5,000 per month from 25 to 45, then left to grow until 60): ₹5.5 Crore
- ➢ **Himanshu's** Corpus (₹10,000 per month from 40 to 60): ₹2 Crore

Even though **Amit** invested half of what **Himanshu** did, he ends up with almost 3 times more wealth! That's the magic of compounding. Starting early beats investing more later.

### Example 2: The ₹1 Lakh Experiment

Let's say you invest ₹1,00,000 in a mutual fund that offers 12% annual returns. Below, we compare the growth of your investment under two scenarios:

- ➢ Without Compounding (Simple Interest) – where interest is calculated only on the initial principal.
- ➢ With Compounding (Compound Interest) – where interest is reinvested, leading to exponential growth over time.

## Investment Growth Over Time

| Year | Without Compounding (Simple Interest) | With Compounding (Compound Interest) |
|---|---|---|
| 1 | ₹1,12,000 | ₹1,12,000 |
| 5 | ₹1,60,000 | ₹1,76,234 |
| 10 | ₹2,20,000 | ₹3,10,585 |
| 20 | ₹3,40,000 | ₹9,64,629 |
| 30 | ₹4,60,000 | ₹29,95,992 |

## Key Takeaways

➢ Simple Interest grows linearly, adding ₹12,000 per year.

➢ Compound Interest grows exponentially, as interest is reinvested each year.

➢ Over 30 years, compounding makes your investment grow nearly 6.5 times more than simple interest.

*This demonstrates why starting early and letting your money compound is one of the most powerful wealth-building strategies!*

## Real-Life Stories of Compounding

### *Warren Buffett – The King of Compounding*

Did you know Warren Buffett made 99% of his wealth after the age of 50? The reason? He started investing at 11 and let compounding do its magic. His patience and discipline made him one of the richest men in the world.

## Key Lessons from Compounding

✓ Start early – The sooner you start, the bigger your wealth grows. Even small investments make a huge difference.

✓ Be consistent – Regular investments (like SIPs) ensure long-term success.

✓ Patience is key – The biggest gains come in later years, so stay invested.

✓ Avoid withdrawing early – Breaking investments reduces compounding benefits.

✓ Reinvest dividends – This accelerates your wealth accumulation.

## Conclusion

Compounding is the most powerful tool for wealth creation. The earlier you start, the more time your money has to grow. A disciplined investor who starts early, invests consistently, and stays patient will always win the financial game.

◈ **So, when is the best time to start? Its NOW!**

◈ **Start investing as early as possible and let Time do the magic!**

## Overview of the Retirement Planning Process

Retirement planning in India doesn't have to be complicated. By breaking down the process into digestible steps, it becomes easier to navigate. Below are the key steps involved:

- ➤ **Assess Your Current Financial Situation**: This includes evaluating your income, savings, investments, and liabilities. Knowing where you stand financially helps you figure out how much you need to save for retirement.

- ➤ **Determine Your Retirement Goals**: Think about the lifestyle you want after retirement: Will you travel? Do you plan to stay in a metropolitan city, or live in a smaller town? Your retirement expenses will be shaped by these choices.

- ➤ **Estimate Your Retirement Corpus**: Estimate the amount you will need when you retire. This involves considering your life expectancy, inflation rates, healthcare costs, and desired lifestyle.

- ➤ **Choose the Right Investment Vehicles**: In India, there are several tax-efficient investment options, such as **Equity-Linked Savings Schemes (ELSS), PPF, National Pension Scheme (NPS),** and **EPF**. Selecting the right vehicle based on your risk tolerance is essential to meeting your retirement goals.

- ➤ **Monitor and Adjust Your Plan**: As you get closer to retirement, your asset allocation should become more conservative. Monitoring your investments and adjusting your plan for changes in income or expenses is crucial.

**Example:**

Here's an example to give you a better perspective:

**Kunal's Retirement Planning Strategy:**

- ➤ Age: 30
- ➤ Monthly Savings: ₹20,000
- ➤ Investment Option: 70% in Equity Mutual Funds (high growth potential) and 30% in PPF (low-risk, tax-advantaged)
- ➤ Expected Rate of Return: 12% *
- ➤ Retirement Age: 60
- ➤ Corpus Goal: ₹ 6 Crore+* (based on current lifestyle and inflation-adjusted needs)

By investing ₹20,000 per month in a combination of equity and PPF, **Kunal** will have a retirement corpus of ₹ 6 Crore+* in 30 years, which would allow him to live comfortably without worrying about money.

**Key Take aways:**

- ➤ Retirement planning is essential for ensuring financial security after your working years.
- ➤ Starting early and being consistent in your savings and investments gives you an edge.
- ➤ It's crucial to estimate your needs and select the right investment vehicles.
- ➤ A well-thought-out retirement plan can help you live the life you want, even after your active working years.

*"A good retirement plan is built on small, consistent actions over time, not on sudden windfalls."* – *Anurag*

## Chapter 2:
# Understanding Your Retirement Needs

**Estimating Retirement Expenses**

One of the most critical aspects of retirement planning is understanding how much money you'll need when you retire. To make an informed estimate, it's crucial to assess your current and future expenses. While some expenses will remain constant, others may increase, particularly healthcare costs.

**Basic Categories of Retirement Expenses**

- ➢ **Lifestyle Expenses:** This includes the costs related to your daily life, such as housing, food, transportation, and leisure. These expenses are often the largest part of your retirement budget.

- ➢ **Healthcare Expenses:** Healthcare becomes more critical as we age. In India, healthcare costs are rising, and expenses for treatments or hospitalization can be significant. Having health insurance or a separate emergency healthcare fund becomes vital in retirement.

- ➢ **Inflation:** Inflation affects the purchasing power of money, which means your expenses will likely increase over time. Even though India has seen moderate inflation in recent years, it's important to account for it when planning for retirement.

➤ **Taxes:** Although income tax may reduce once you retire (depending on the type of income), certain expenditures (such as capital gains from investments) can still attract taxes. Planning for tax efficiency in your retirement income is crucial.

## Lifestyle Choices: What Do You Want to Do After Retirement?

In India, retirement often means a shift in lifestyle. Some people may choose to live in a bigger city, while others may prefer a quieter life in a smaller town or village. Some might want to travel the world, while others may simply want to spend time with family or engage in hobbies.

## Important Questions to Consider:

➤ **Where will you live?** Costs of living in cities like Mumbai or Delhi can be much higher than in smaller towns or rural areas. Think about whether you want to stay in the same place or relocate post-retirement.

➤ **What kind of healthcare will you need?** As you age, healthcare becomes a priority. Consider the cost of medical insurance or long-term care.

➤ **Do you want to travel?** For many, retirement is a time to explore the world, but travel can be expensive. Budgeting for this can help ensure you don't run out of money while pursuing your dream adventures.

## Healthcare and Medical Costs in India

Healthcare costs in India are rising, and the Indian government's healthcare schemes like **Ayushman Bharat** may not cover all your needs. Private healthcare, while of high quality, can be expensive, and out-of-pocket expenses may deplete your retirement savings if not planned for.

## Factors to Consider:

- **Medical Insurance:** Many Indians rely on family or employer-provided insurance during their working years. However, post-retirement, you'll need to purchase an individual or family health insurance policy. Look for policies that cover critical illnesses and hospitalization expenses.

- **Long-Term Care:** Long-term care facilities (for conditions like Alzheimer's or dementia) are expensive in India. While this may not be a concern at the start of retirement, it's crucial to consider this as part of your long-term planning.

- **Age-related Medical Costs:** For retirees, expenses on medications, doctor's visits, and diagnostic tests can increase significantly as they age.

## Example:

Let's take ***Vaidan*t** and ***Riya***, who are planning for their retirement:

- **Vaidant (age 45)** and **Riya (age 43)** both have a family history of diabetes and Pre-existing disease(PED). They decide to include ₹5,000 per month for medical insurance and a separate emergency healthcare fund of ₹10 lakh by the time they turn 60.

> By contributing a modest amount every year to a health savings account, **Vaidant** and **Riya** ensure they are covered for unexpected medical expenses when they retire.

## Inflation and Its Impact on Retirement Planning

Inflation is one of the biggest risks to your retirement savings, and in India, inflation can vary across different sectors. While food prices may rise quickly, some areas (like education or luxury items) may experience even faster inflation.

## How to Account for Inflation in Retirement Planning:

> **Annual Inflation Rate:** India's inflation rate has averaged around 6-7% in the past decade. However, for retirement planning, it's safer to assume an inflation rate of 7-8% to account for fluctuations.

> **Inflation's Effect on Expenses:** If your current monthly expenses are ₹50,000, in 20 years (with an inflation rate of 7%), those expenses will rise to ₹1,90,000 per month. This illustrates how critical it is to plan ahead.

## Example:

**Monika** is 40 years old and expects to retire at 60. She currently spends ₹50,000 per month, but assuming an inflation rate of 7%, her monthly expenses will rise to ₹1,20,000 by the time she retires. That's an increase of 140% in her expense needs.

To account for this, **Monika** adjusts her savings strategy by allocating a higher percentage of her income to retirement savings.

## Estimating the Retirement Corpus

To calculate how much money you'll need in retirement, it's essential to estimate your desired monthly expenses and consider inflation over the years. Below is a simple method for calculating your retirement corpus:

- ➢ **Estimate Monthly Expenses:** Start by calculating how much you'll spend each month during retirement.
- ➢ **Account for Inflation:** Use the formula for future value to adjust your expenses for inflation.
- ➢ **Multiply by 12:** Once you have your annual expenses, multiply by 12 to get your yearly expenses.
- ➢ **Multiply by Number of Years in Retirement:** Estimate how many years you'll need to cover expenses (based on life expectancy).

## Example:

Let's look at *Amit* and *Sonia*:

- ➢ Current Monthly Expenses: ₹60,000
- ➢ Desired Monthly Expenses in Retirement (at age 60): ₹1,20,000 (due to inflation)
- ➢ Retirement Duration: 25 years

## Corpus Required:

- ➢ **Annual Expenses:** ₹1,20,000 x 12 = ₹14,40,000
- ➢ **Retirement Corpus:** ₹14,40,000 x 25 = ₹3.6 Crores

In this case, **Amit** and **Sonia** will need a corpus of ₹3.6 Crores* by the time they retire to maintain their lifestyle without financial strain.

**Key Takeaways:**

- Estimating your retirement expenses and adjusting for inflation is crucial.

- Healthcare costs will likely increase with age, so it's important to budget for insurance and medical expenses.

- Understanding your desired lifestyle and location can help you estimate your future costs.

- Inflation can significantly impact your retirement savings; plan accordingly.

*"**Retirement planning is like a marathon, not a sprint.**"* – *Anurag*

## Chapter 3:
# Retirement Goals and Setting Milestones

### Setting Clear Retirement Goals

Retirement goals serve as the foundation of your retirement planning. In India, a common misconception is that retirement simply means stopping work and enjoying life without considering the finances required for it. However, retirement planning goes beyond just quitting your job—it involves setting financial goals that ensure a comfortable life when you no longer have a regular pay check.

### Key Considerations When Setting Retirement Goals:

- **Desired Lifestyle**: Your lifestyle after retirement will significantly influence how much you need to save. Will you continue living in a metropolitan city like Mumbai, Delhi, & Bangalore where the cost of living is higher, or will you relocate to a quieter, more affordable city? Do you want to travel the world or focus on hobbies? These choices will determine your retirement expenses.

- **Time Horizon**: The time you have before retirement plays a major role in how aggressively you should invest. The longer you have, the more your investments can grow due to compound interest.

➢ **Retirement Age and Life Expectancy**: The age at which you plan to retire and your expected life expectancy will determine how long you need your retirement savings to last. In India, life expectancy is increasing, so you might need to plan for a retirement lasting 30 years or more.

**Example:**

**Kartik** (30 years) and **Shruti** (28 years) want to retire at 60. They plan to spend ₹80,000 per month after retirement, and they expect to live until 85. Their financial goal is to save enough to cover 25 years of expenses post-retirement, taking into account inflation.

**Kartik and Shruti Key Goal:**

➢ Monthly expenses after retirement: ₹80,000

➢ Total expenses for 25 years: ₹80,000 x 12 months x 25 years = ₹2.4 Crores

➢ Considering inflation of 7%, they need to adjust this amount upwards to ₹ 3 Crores.

## *The SMART Method for Goal Setting*

A structured way to set your retirement goals is by using the **SMART** method, which ensures that your goals are ***Specific, Measurable, Achievable, Relevant, and Time-bound***. This approach helps you break down big goals into smaller, manageable tasks.

**Breaking Down the SMART Framework:**

- **Specific**: A clear, well-defined goal helps focus efforts. For example, instead of saying "I want to be rich," say, "I want to accumulate ₹ 10 crore by age 60 for retirement."

- **Measurable**: It's important to measure your progress. For example, you can measure your goal by tracking the corpus you need for retirement or the monthly savings required to achieve that corpus.

- **Achievable**: Ensure your goals are realistic based on your current financial situation. If you currently earn ₹20 lakh a year, setting a goal of ₹10 crore in 5 years might not be feasible unless you increase your income or savings substantially.

- **Relevant**: Your goal should align with your long-term vision for retirement. For example, if your goal is to travel the world after retirement, you'll need to save more compared to someone who plans to stay in their home country with minimal travel.

- **Time-bound**: A specific time frame helps keep you on track. For example, "I want to accumulate ₹ 10 crore for retirement by the time I turn 50."

## Example of SMART Goals in Retirement Planning:

- ➢ **Specific:** "I want to accumulate ₹ 10 crore by age 60 for retirement."

- ➢ **Measurable:** "I will save ₹50,000 per month towards retirement for the next 20 years."

- ➢ **Achievable:** "Given my current income and expenses, saving ₹50,000 monthly is feasible."

- ➢ **Relevant:** "This goal supports my plan to retire at 60 and live comfortably in a smaller city."

- ➢ **Time-bound:** "I will achieve my goal of ₹ 10 crore by age 60."

## Evaluating Your Current Financial Situation

Before setting goals, it's essential to evaluate your current financial situation. In India, many individuals have various savings and investment accounts, but these might not be aligned with their retirement goals. Here's how to evaluate your current financial health:

- ➢ **Income:** How much are you earning currently? Consider all sources of income, including salary, rental income, business income, and interest on savings.

- ➢ **Expenses:** What are your monthly expenses? How much do you save and invest? Are you overspending in certain areas? Tracking your expenses will help you determine how much you can allocate toward retirement savings.

- ➢ **Debt:** Do you have any outstanding loans, such as a home loan, car loan, or personal loan? Debt payments can take a big chunk out of your retirement savings, so it's important to address and manage it effectively.

➢ **Assets:** Assess your current assets, including savings accounts, mutual funds, PPF, EPF, gold, property, and other investments. Are they growing in line with your retirement goals?

## Setting Retirement Milestones

Once your retirement goal is clear, breaking it down into smaller milestones can help track progress and motivate you to stay on course. Milestones should be based on your target retirement age (60, for example) and should align with your life stages.

## Example:

**Barun** (35 years) is planning to retire at 60. His goal is to accumulate ₹ 10 Crore for retirement.

To reach this goal, he breaks down his retirement milestones:

- ➢ **At 40 years:** Save ₹50 lakh
- ➢ **At 45 years:** Save ₹ 2 crore
- ➢ **At 50 years:** Save ₹ 5 crore
- ➢ **At 55 years:** Save ₹7.5 crore
- ➢ **At 60 years:** Achieve ₹10 crore

Each milestone helps **Barun** to track his progress and adjust his savings and investment strategy if needed.

## Tools for Tracking Retirement Milestones

To track your retirement progress effectively, you can use the following tools:

- ➢ **Retirement Calculators:** These online tools help estimate the amount of money you'll need based on your current expenses, inflation rate, and expected returns on investments.

- ➢ **Investment Portfolio:** Regularly monitor your investments to ensure they are aligned with your risk profile and financial goals.

- ➢ **Budgeting Tools:** Use budgeting apps or spreadsheets to track your income and expenses, ensuring you can allocate the right amount to your retirement fund.

## Key Take aways:

- ➢ Setting clear, measurable, and time-bound retirement goals is essential for success.

- ➢ The *SMART* method helps break down retirement planning into achievable steps.

- ➢ Assessing your current financial situation is a crucial step before setting goals.

- ➢ Setting milestones helps you track progress and stay motivated to achieve your retirement goals.

*"The earlier you start, the easier it gets. The longer you wait, the harder it becomes."* – Anurag

## Chapter 4:
# Investment Strategies for Retirement

**The Importance of Investing for Retirement**

Saving for retirement is important, but investing for retirement is what can help you accumulate the wealth needed to maintain your desired lifestyle. Simply saving money in a bank account or traditional savings plan may not yield the returns needed to beat inflation and ensure a financially secure retirement.

**Why Invest?**

- ➢ **Combat Inflation:** The rising cost of living means that your savings today won't have the same purchasing power in the future. Investing allows you to grow your money faster than inflation.

- ➢ **Wealth Accumulation:** Investments such as stocks, mutual funds, and real estate can provide higher returns compared to traditional savings accounts.

- ➢ **Tax Efficiency:** Many investments options offer tax-saving opportunities that reduce your tax liability today, while simultaneously building a retirement corpus for the future.

## 1. Equities (Stocks & Mutual Funds) – Growth and Risk

Investing in **equities** or stocks & Mutual Funds is one of the most popular ways to build wealth for retirement. While equities have the potential to provide high returns, they also come with higher risk due to market volatility.

**Key Features of Equities:**

- **High Returns:** Over the long term, equities typically offer returns higher than inflation, making them an essential component of a retirement portfolio.

- **Volatility:** While equities can generate high returns, they are also subject to market swings. Therefore, investing in stocks requires a long-term perspective and the ability to withstand short-term volatility.

- **Dividend Income:** Some companies pay dividends, which can provide a regular source of income during retirement.

**Example:**

**Neeraj** invests ₹10,000 every month in a mix of large-cap and mid-cap Mutual Funds through a **Systematic Investment Plan (SIP)**. Over 20 years, his portfolio grows at an average annual return of 12%, significantly increasing his retirement corpus.

## 2. Mutual Funds – Diversification and Professional Management

**Mutual funds** pool money from multiple investors to invest in a diversified portfolio of stocks, bonds, or other assets. They are an excellent option for people who want to invest in the equity or debt markets but lack the expertise to select individual stocks.

## Key Features of Mutual Funds:

- **Diversification:** Mutual funds invest in a wide variety of assets, helping to reduce risk by spreading investments across different sectors or asset classes.

- **Professional Management:** A fund manager actively manages the investments, making decisions on behalf of the investors.

- **Different Types of Funds:** There are various types of mutual funds, such as **equity mutual funds**, **debt mutual funds**, and **hybrid funds**.

## Example:

**Divya** decides to invest ₹10,000 per month in an equity mutual fund that targets high-growth companies. Over time, her investment grows at an average annual return of 12%, providing her with a growing retirement fund.

## 3. Fixed Income Securities – Stability and Safety

While equities and mutual funds offer higher returns, they come with higher risk. If you are risk-averse or closer to retirement, **fixed income securities** such as **bonds** or **fixed deposits (FDs)** can provide stability and safety for your portfolio.

## Key Features of Fixed Income Investments:

- **Stability:** Fixed income investments provide predictable returns through interest payments, offering more stability than equities.

- **Lower Risk:** They are generally less volatile and can provide a steady income stream, making them ideal for retirees.

- **Interest Rate Risk:** Interest rates have an inverse relationship with bond prices—when interest rates rise, bond prices fall. This can affect the value of your bond investments.

**Example:**

**Anjali** prefers low-risk investments and invests ₹10,000 monthly in a **government bond** with an interest rate of 7%. This investment grows steadily over time and provides her with stable returns.

### 4. Real Estate – Tangible Asset for Wealth Creation

**Real estate** can be a great long-term investment, offering both potential for capital appreciation and rental income. Although it may require a larger initial investment, it can significantly contribute to your retirement corpus.

### Key Features of Real Estate:

- **Capital Appreciation:** Real estate generally appreciates in value over time, offering significant returns when you sell the property.

- **Rental Income:** Real estate can also provide regular rental income, which can be a steady source of funds during retirement.

- **Low Liquidity:** Unlike stocks or mutual funds, real estate is not a highly liquid investment, meaning it may take time to sell if you need access to cash quickly.

**Example:**

**Shivam** invests in a residential property in a growing area. Over 15 years, the property's value appreciates, and he also earns rental income, providing him with both capital gains and regular income during his retirement.

## 5. Gold – Safe-Haven Asset

**Gold** is considered a safe-haven investment, especially during times of economic uncertainty. It is often used as a hedge against inflation and market volatility.

**Key Features of Gold:**

- **Hedge Against Inflation:** Gold typically holds its value over time and can increase in value during periods of inflation.
- **Liquidity:** Gold is a highly liquid asset, meaning it can be sold quickly if needed.
- **Physical vs Digital Gold:** You can invest in physical gold (coins, bars, jewellery) or financial gold (gold ETFs or sovereign gold bonds).

**Example:**

**Miraya** invests in **Sovereign Gold Bonds (SGBs)**, which offer both capital appreciation and annual interest, as well as tax benefits. Over time, her investment in gold appreciates and provides a safe, stable addition to her retirement corpus.

## 6. Systematic Investment Plan (SIP) – Consistency and Discipline

A **Systematic Investment Plan (SIP)** is a disciplined way to invest in mutual funds. SIPs allow you to invest a fixed amount regularly, helping you average out the cost of your investments over time.

**Key Features of SIP:**

- **Regular Contributions:** SIPs encourage you to invest a fixed amount each month, ensuring consistent contributions to your retirement fund.

- ➢ **Rupee -Cost Averaging:** SIPs help reduce the impact of market volatility by investing a fixed amount, whether the market is up or down.
- ➢ **Compounding:** SIPs harness the power of compounding, helping your investments grow exponentially over time.

**Example:**

**Amit** invests ₹20,000 every month through an SIP in a diversified equity fund. Over 25 years, his investment grows significantly due to the compounding effect.

**Asset Allocation: Building a Balanced Portfolio**

A key principle of investment for retirement is **asset allocation**, which refers to how you distribute your investments among different asset classes—such as equities, bonds, real estate, and gold. The right allocation depends on your risk tolerance, time horizon, and financial goals.

**How to Build a Balanced Portfolio:**

- ➢ **Younger Investors (20s-30s):** Focus on equities and mutual funds for high growth, with a small portion in safer assets like bonds.
- ➢ **Mid-Life Investors (40s-50s):** Shift towards a more balanced portfolio with equities for growth and fixed-income investments for stability.
- ➢ **Pre-Retirement and Retirees (60+):** Prioritize safe investments like bonds, real estate, and annuities, while maintaining some growth-oriented investments.

**Example of Asset Allocation:**

**Kunal** (age 40) follows a 60% equity, 30% fixed-income, and 10% gold allocation strategy to maximize returns while minimizing risk. As he approaches retirement age, he gradually shifts towards a more conservative allocation with 40% in equity, 50% in bonds, and 10% in gold.

**Key Takeaways:**

- **Equities** offer high returns but come with higher risk. They are best suited for long-term investors with a high-risk tolerance.

- **Mutual Funds** provide diversification and professional management, making them a good option for both beginners and experienced investors.

- **Fixed Income Securities** offer stability and are suitable for those seeking lower risk and predictable returns.

- **Real Estate** can be a solid investment for those looking for long-term growth and rental income.

- **Gold** acts as a safe-haven asset and helps hedge against inflation.

- **SIPs** provide a disciplined way to invest regularly and harness the power of compounding.

- **Asset Allocation** is key to managing risk and achieving balanced growth in your retirement portfolio.

*"Retirement is not about the end of your work life; it's about creating a life that you love, financially prepared for what's to come."* – *Anurag*

## Chapter 5:
# Tax Planning for Retirement

**Overview of Tax Planning for Retirement**

Effective tax planning is an essential part of retirement planning. In India, various retirement accounts and investment instruments offer tax-saving benefits, allowing you to grow your retirement savings faster while reducing your tax liability. Understanding how to optimize your tax planning will ensure that more of your money goes toward building your retirement corpus.

**1. Tax Benefits of Retirement Accounts**

Certain retirement accounts and investment schemes offer tax-saving opportunities that can significantly reduce your taxable income. Let's explore the most common options available in India.

**Employees' Provident Fund (EPF)**

The **EPF** is one of the most tax-efficient retirement saving schemes in India. Contributions to the EPF, along with interest earned, are tax-free.

> ➢ **Tax Deduction on Contributions:** The contributions made to EPF are eligible for tax deductions under **Section 80C**. The maximum limit for deductions under Section 80C is ₹1.5 lakh per financial year.

- **Tax-Free Interest:** The interest earned on the EPF balance is tax-free, making it an attractive long-term retirement saving option.

- **Tax-Free Maturity Amount:** At the time of withdrawal, the maturity amount is tax-free, provided the employee has completed at least five years of service.

**Example:**

If you contribute ₹1 lakh annually to your EPF, you can claim a tax deduction of ₹1 lakh under Section 80C. The interest earned and the amount received upon maturity will be completely tax-free.

**Public Provident Fund (PPF)**

The **PPF** is another popular tax-saving instrument. It is known for its safety and tax-free returns.

- **Tax Deduction on Contributions:** Contributions to the PPF are eligible for tax deductions under **Section 80C**, up to ₹1.5 lakh annually.

- **Tax-Free Interest:** The interest earned on PPF is tax-free, and withdrawals made after the 15-year maturity period are also tax-free.

- **Tax-Free Maturity Amount:** The maturity amount, including both the principal and interest, is tax-free.

**Example:**

If you invest ₹1.5 lakh annually in a PPF account, you can avail of a tax deduction of ₹1.5 lakh under Section 80C. The interest earned and the corpus at maturity will not be taxed.

## National Pension Scheme (NPS)

The **National Pension Scheme (NPS)** offers substantial tax benefits, especially if you are looking to save for retirement while lowering your tax liability.

- ➤ **Tax Deduction on Contributions:** Contributions to NPS are eligible for tax deductions under **Section 80C** (up to ₹1.5 lakh). Additionally, under **Section 80CCD(1B)**, you can claim an additional ₹50,000 in tax deductions for contributions to NPS. This makes NPS one of the best tax-saving instruments for retirement planning.

- ➤ **Tax-Deferred Growth:** The contributions made to NPS grow tax-deferred, meaning you don't have to pay tax on the capital gains earned in your NPS account until you make withdrawals.

- ➤ **Tax-Free Annuity Option:** At the time of retirement, you are required to use a portion of the corpus to purchase an annuity. The annuity payments are subject to tax, but the initial corpus is tax-free.

## Example:

If you contribute ₹50,000 annually to NPS, you can claim a deduction under Section 80C for ₹1.5 lakh and an additional deduction of ₹50,000 under Section 80CCD(1B). This means you can save ₹50,000 more in taxes while building your retirement savings.

## 2. Maximizing Tax Savings Using Section 80C

**Section 80C** of the Income Tax Act allows for deductions up to ₹1.5 lakh per financial year on certain investments. While most retirement plans already provide tax benefits under this section, you can further optimize your tax savings by combining various eligible options.

**Tax-Saving Investments Under Section 80C:**

- **EPF and VPF Contributions:** Contributions to the Employees' Provident Fund (EPF) and Voluntary Provident Fund (VPF) are eligible for deductions.

- **PPF Contributions:** As mentioned, PPF contributions are also eligible under Section 80C.

- **Tax-Saving Fixed Deposits (FDs):** If you opt for a 5-year tax-saving fixed deposit, you can claim a deduction under Section 80C.

- **National Savings Certificates (NSC):** NSCs are also eligible for deductions under Section 80C.

- **Sukanya Samriddhi Yojana (SSY):** Contributions to the SSY are eligible for deductions under Section 80C, making it an excellent option for retirement planning if you have a daughter.

**Example:**

By investing in PPF, EPF, and NSC, you can reach the ₹1.5 lakh limit for tax-saving under Section 80C while simultaneously building your retirement corpus.

### 3. Tax-Free Income from Long-Term Investments

When investing for retirement, it's important to consider options that allow you to earn tax-free income. Some of the most popular tax-free investment options include:

- **PPF:** The interest earned and maturity amount are completely tax-free.

- **NPS:** While the initial corpus is tax-free, the annuity is subject to tax.

> **Sovereign Gold Bonds (SGBs):** The interest earned on SGBs is taxable, but the capital gains at maturity are tax-free.

> **Tax-Free Bonds:** Certain government-backed bonds provide tax-free interest income, making them an attractive option for retirement planning.

**Example:**

If you invest in **Sovereign Gold Bonds** for long-term growth, you can earn interest annually, and when you sell them after maturity, the capital gains will be tax-free.

### 4. Tax Planning for Retirees

Once you approach retirement, your tax planning strategy should shift to focus on managing income tax on your retirement benefits. Here are some tax-saving tips for retirees:

**Tax-Free Retirement Income Options:**

> **Senior Citizens Savings Scheme (SCSS):** If you are over 60 years old, the interest earned on SCSS is taxable, but the principal invested is exempt from tax.

> **Reverse Mortgage Loans:** This option allows retirees to convert their home equity into a stream of income. The proceeds from a reverse mortgage loan are not considered taxable income.

> **Annuities:** Annuity income is subject to tax based on your tax slab, but if you invest in an annuity for your retirement, you can spread your tax liability over time.

**Tax-Free Withdrawals:**

> **EPF and PPF Maturity:** Withdrawals from EPF and PPF are tax-free when the individual meets the required conditions (such as the number of years of service or the 15-year lock-in period for PPF).

> **NPS Withdrawals:** A portion of your NPS corpus must be used to purchase an annuity, and the annuity income is taxed. However, the portion of the corpus withdrawn as a lump sum is tax-free.

**Example:**

After retirement, **Akshat** invests his lump sum retirement amount in tax-free bonds, and his rental income from a property is also tax-free. This allows him to have a steady and tax-efficient income in retirement.

## 5. Tax Planning for Post-Retirement Withdrawal

Once you start withdrawing from your retirement accounts, the tax implications may vary depending on the type of account and your income tax slab. Here are some key tax considerations:

> **EPF and PPF Withdrawals:** Both EPF and PPF withdrawals are tax-free after a certain lock-in period.

> **NPS Withdrawals:** A portion of the NPS corpus must be used to buy an annuity, which is taxable. However, you can choose the amount you wish to withdraw, and the lump sum portion is tax-free.

> **Capital Gains Tax on Real Estate:** If you sell a property before three years, it will be subject to short-term capital gains tax. If sold after three years, the long-term capital gains tax will apply, which can

be reduced by investing in specified bonds under Section 54EC.

**Example:**

**Ashish** plans to withdraw from his PPF account after 15 years, making his withdrawal tax-free. He also plans to sell his old property, and since it is a long-term capital asset, he benefits from reduced tax on the capital gains.

**Key Takeaways:**

- **Retirement Accounts** like EPF, PPF, and NPS offer significant tax-saving opportunities, reducing your tax liability while growing your retirement savings.

- **Section 80C** provides tax deductions on contributions to retirement and tax-saving schemes, helping you optimize your savings.

- **Long-Term Investments** such as PPF, NPS, and Sovereign Gold Bonds provide tax-free income, allowing your savings to grow faster.

- As you approach **retirement**, focus on managing your income tax through strategic withdrawals and tax-free income options.

*"Financial freedom is a key to retirement, but planning is the lock that opens the door."* – *Anurag*

## Chapter 6:
# Creating a Retirement Budget

**Why is a Retirement Budget Important?**

A well-thought-out retirement budget is crucial because it allows you to assess your future financial needs, track your expenses, and ensure that your retirement corpus lasts as long as you do. Without a clear budget, you may run the risk of overspending or underestimating your financial requirements, which could affect your lifestyle in retirement.

Creating a retirement budget ensures that you:

- Have enough funds for your desired lifestyle.
- Plan for unexpected expenses.
- Avoid running out of money too early in retirement.
- Align your retirement goals with your available resources.

**1. Estimating Your Retirement Expenses**

The first step in creating a retirement budget is estimating how much money you will need each month and year to maintain your lifestyle during retirement. While some expenses may decrease (like work-related costs), others may increase (like healthcare expenses).

## Common Expenses in Retirement:

- ➢ **Basic Living Expenses:** Food, clothing, utilities, transportation, and other day-to-day needs.
- ➢ **Housing:** Rent or mortgage payments, property taxes, maintenance, and insurance.
- ➢ **Healthcare:** Medical insurance premiums, medical treatments, medications, and doctor visits.
- ➢ **Leisure and Entertainment:** Travel, hobbies, dining out, and other recreational activities.
- ➢ **Taxes:** Income taxes on pension, social security benefits, or any other income generated in retirement.
- ➢ **Emergency Fund:** Setting aside funds for unforeseen events, like home repairs or family emergencies.

## Example:

- ➢ **Shivam** estimates his monthly expenses at ₹ 1,00,000, which includes:
  - ₹ 30,000 for housing (rent)
  - ₹ 20,000 for food and utilities
  - ₹ 10,000 for healthcare
  - ₹ 20,000 for leisure and entertainment
  - ₹ 15,000 for transportation
  - ₹5,000 for miscellaneous and emergency expenses This means his annual expenses will amount to ₹ 12 lakh.

## 2. Understanding the 70-80% Rule

A common rule of thumb when estimating retirement expenses is the **70-80% Rule**. This suggests that you will likely need **70% to 80%** of your pre-retirement income to maintain a similar standard of living during retirement.

### How the Rule Works:

- If your current monthly income is ₹1,00,000, you may need approximately ₹70,000 to ₹80,000 per month in retirement.

- The amount you need will depend on various factors, including how much debt you have, your current living style, and whether you plan to travel or indulge in expensive hobbies during retirement.

### Example:

- If **Amyra** is earning ₹1,20,000 per month before retirement, she may expect to need about ₹96,000 to ₹1,00,000 per month in retirement, which is approximately 80% of her current income.

## 3. Accounting for Inflation

Inflation is the steady increase in prices over time. It erodes the purchasing power of your money, so when planning for retirement, it is crucial to account for inflation in your budget.

### Inflation Impact:

- The cost of goods and services tends to rise at an average annual inflation rate of **6%** in India. This means that what you pay for products and services today will cost more in the future.

- ➢ **Healthcare costs** typically rise faster than the general inflation rate, so budgeting for medical expenses becomes even more important.

**How to Account for Inflation:**

- ➢ Multiply your current annual expenses by the expected inflation rate to determine how much those expenses will increase by the time you retire.

- ➢ For example, if **Amit** is currently spending ₹6,00,000 annually, and the expected inflation rate is 6%, his expenses in 20 years would be approximately ₹19,28,000 annually.

**Example:**

If **Ram** estimates a need of ₹8,00,000 per year in retirement (adjusted for inflation), and he expects to live 30 years in retirement, he needs to save accordingly to cover this cost, factoring in yearly increases.

**4. Determining Your Income Sources in Retirement**

Once you know your expenses, it's essential to identify where your income will come from during retirement. Common sources of income include:

**Sources of Retirement Income:**

- ➢ **Pension:** If your employer provides a pension plan, it may offer a fixed monthly income for life.

- ➢ **EPF & Gratuity:** Your provident fund or gratuity payout could provide a lump sum that you can withdraw periodically for retirement income.

- ➢ **Mutual Fund SIPs & Investments:** Income generated from systematic withdrawal plans (SWPs) or dividends from investments.

- ➢ **Rental Income:** If you own property, rental income can provide a steady stream of cash.

- ➢ **Annuities:** Fixed monthly payouts from annuities purchased with part of your retirement corpus.

- ➢ **Part-Time Work or Freelancing:** Some retirees prefer to work part-time or consult, generating additional income.

**Example:**

- ➢ **Ravi** has a pension plan that will provide him with ₹40,000 per month, and he also expects to receive ₹15,000 per month from his rental property. He needs to generate an additional ₹35,000 per month through his investments to meet his retirement goals.

**5. Balancing Your Budget: Managing Surplus and Deficit**

Once you have a rough idea of your monthly income and expenses, compare them to see if there's a surplus or deficit. This will help you decide how much you need to save or adjust in your retirement planning.

**In Case of a Deficit:**

- ➢ **Cutting Expenses:** Identify areas where you can reduce costs, such as leisure activities or expensive hobbies.

- ➢ **Increasing Savings:** You may need to save more during your working years or find additional income sources in retirement, like part-time work.

**In Case of a Surplus:**

- ➢ **Reinvesting Excess Funds:** Consider reinvesting any surplus income into high-yield investments, such as mutual funds, to grow your retirement corpus.

> **Building Emergency Fund:** Ensure that you have a sufficient emergency fund in place to cover unexpected medical or financial emergencies.

**Example:**

> **Vanshika** has ₹80,000 in monthly expenses and ₹1,00,000 in monthly income from her pension and rental income. With a surplus of ₹20,000 per month, she decides to reinvest it into Moderate-risk Hybrid funds to ensure a growing corpus for her later years.

## 6. Planning for Healthcare and Medical Expenses

Healthcare becomes an increasingly significant expense in retirement, so budgeting for medical costs is essential. In India, healthcare costs have been rising at a faster rate than inflation, and medical insurance becomes an important part of retirement planning.

### Healthcare Budgeting Tips:

> **Health Insurance:** Secure comprehensive health insurance that covers hospitalization, surgeries, and chronic disease management. Ensure that the policy covers you until advanced age.

> **Medical Emergency Fund:** Set aside a separate fund for medical emergencies, especially if you have existing health conditions.

> **Long-Term Care:** As you age, you may require long-term care or assisted living. Factor this into your retirement planning.

**Example:**

> **Deepak** includes ₹20,000 per month in his retirement budget for medical insurance premiums, doctor visits, and medications.

## 7. Tracking and Adjusting Your Budget Over Time

Your retirement budget will evolve over time. Tracking your expenses regularly and adjusting for changes in income, lifestyle, or unforeseen expenses is essential for maintaining financial stability.

**Budget Tracking Tips:**

- Use budget tracking apps or spreadsheets to monitor your monthly expenses and income.
- Review your retirement budget annually and adjust for inflation, changes in medical costs, or unexpected life events.
- Consider working with a financial advisor to make any necessary adjustments to your retirement plan.

**Key Takeaways:**

- A **retirement budget** is essential to ensure that you can meet your financial needs in retirement without running out of funds.
- Estimate your **retirement expenses** carefully, accounting for inflation, healthcare, and unforeseen costs.
- Identify your **income sources**, such as pensions, investments, and rental income, to meet your estimated expenses.
- Plan for potential **healthcare costs** and track your budget regularly to ensure you stay on track with your goals.

*"Retirement planning is the process of setting yourself up for a future where you have the freedom to live the life you want, without financial stress."* – *Anurag*

## Chapter 7:
# Managing Post-Retirement Income

**The Challenge of Managing Retirement Income**

Once you retire, the dynamics of your finances change. Instead of earning a regular pay check, your income will now come from the savings and investments you've accumulated over the years. The key challenge in this phase is ensuring that your money lasts throughout your retirement years while maintaining your desired standard of living.

It's crucial to take a strategic approach to manage your post-retirement income, focusing on creating a sustainable income stream and ensuring that your financial security isn't compromised.

**1. Understanding Your Retirement Income Sources**

The first step in managing post-retirement income is identifying the sources of income you will rely on. These could include:

**Common Sources of Post-Retirement Income:**

> - **Pension Plans:** If you are eligible for a pension, this will be a regular monthly income.
>
> - **Social Security or Government Benefits:** In India, this may include schemes like the **Pradhan Mantri**

**Shram Yogi Maandhan Yojana**, which offers a monthly pension for unorganized sector workers.

- **Mutual Fund SWPs (Systematic Withdrawal Plans):** A strategy to withdraw a fixed sum from your mutual fund investments periodically.

- **Fixed Deposits & Bonds:** Interest earned from fixed deposits, bonds, or other low-risk instruments can provide stable income.

- **Rental Income:** If you own property, rental income can serve as an additional income stream.

- **Annuities:** An annuity is a financial product that guarantees regular payouts for a specified period or for life, providing a steady income stream.

**Example:**

- **Mohit** has a combination of **pension income** (₹30,000 per month),

- **Rental income** (₹20,000 per month), and plans to withdraw ₹40,000 per month from his **mutual fund SWP**.

## 2. Creating a Sustainable Withdrawal Strategy

One of the biggest challenges in retirement is deciding how much to withdraw from your savings each month. Withdraw too much, and you risk depleting your funds too soon. Withdraw too little, and you may not enjoy the quality of life you desire.

**Key Strategies for Withdrawal:**

➢ **The 6% Rule:** This rule suggests withdrawing 6% of your initial retirement corpus each year. For example, if you have ₹1 crore in savings, you can safely withdraw ₹6 lakh in the first year of retirement. After that, you adjust this amount for inflation.

➢ **Systematic Withdrawal Plans (SWP):** This involves withdrawing a fixed amount at regular intervals (monthly, quarterly, or yearly). This ensures a steady income stream while your investment continues to grow.

➢ **Income-Producing Investments:** Consider keeping a portion of your portfolio in income-producing assets like bonds, fixed deposits, and dividend-paying stocks. These can generate regular income without needing to sell off assets.

➢ **Consider a Ladder Strategy:** If you're relying on fixed-income products (like fixed deposits or bonds), you can create a "ladder" strategy by investing in instruments with different maturity periods. This strategy helps you balance liquidity and higher returns.

**Example:**

➢ **Ekta**, who has ₹50 lakh saved up for retirement, opts for a **6 % withdrawal strategy**, withdrawing ₹ 3 lakh per year in the first year. Additionally, she sets up an **SWP** of ₹25,000 per month from her equity mutual funds.

## 3. Managing Taxes on Post-Retirement Income

Taxes continue to be an important consideration even after retirement. Managing taxes can help you retain a larger portion of your retirement income, allowing your savings to last longer.

**Tax Considerations:**

- **Interest on Fixed Deposits:** The interest earned from fixed deposits is taxable at your applicable tax rate. If your income exceeds the exemption limit, you may need to pay tax on the interest earned.

- **Withdrawals from EPF or NPS:** While **NPS** withdrawals are generally tax-free upon retirement, contributions to the **EPF** are tax-deferred, and you may have to pay tax on the interest earned during your retirement years.

- **Rental Income:** Income from rental property is taxable under the head "Income from House Property." You can claim deductions for property tax, interest on home loans, and repairs, which can reduce your taxable income.

- **Capital Gains Tax on Mutual Funds:** If you sell your mutual fund units, you may incur capital gains tax. The rate depends on the duration you hold the funds and whether they are equity or debt mutual funds.

**Example:**

- **Neeraj**, after retiring, receives ₹15,000 per month from fixed deposits, but the interest is taxable. He explores tax-saving options such as **Senior Citizens' Savings Scheme (SCSS)** and **Post Office Monthly Income Scheme (POMIS)** to minimize taxes.

## 4. Managing Inflation and Rising Costs

As you age, inflation can erode your purchasing power, making it difficult to maintain your lifestyle on a fixed income. This is why it's important to plan for inflation, especially in the long term.

**Inflation-Protection Strategies:**

- **Invest in Growth Assets:** Even in retirement, a portion of your portfolio should be invested in equity funds or other growth assets that can outpace inflation.

- **Annuities with Inflation Adjustment:** Some annuities offer the option of inflation-adjusted payouts. These annuities increase the payout amount annually, helping you keep up with inflation.

- **Review and Adjust Withdrawals:** Each year, review your expenses and the impact of inflation. If your costs are rising faster than expected, you may need to adjust your withdrawal strategy.

**Example:**

- **Ravi** invests 30% of his retirement corpus in **equity mutual funds** to ensure that his investments continue to grow and outpace inflation over time.

## 5. Planning for Healthcare and Long-Term Care Costs

As you get older, healthcare expenses will likely increase. It's crucial to plan for these rising costs to avoid depleting your retirement savings. Additionally, the need for long-term care, such as nursing homes or home healthcare, may arise.

## Healthcare Strategies:

- **Health Insurance:** Ensure that you have comprehensive **health insurance** that covers hospitalization, surgeries, and other medical needs.

- **Critical Illness Insurance:** In addition to regular health insurance, consider critical illness insurance, which covers expensive treatments for serious diseases like cancer or heart conditions.

- **Long-Term Care Insurance:** If you are concerned about long-term care costs, consider purchasing long-term care insurance, which can help cover expenses related to nursing homes, in-home care, or assisted living.

## Example:

- **Payal**, at 60, purchases a comprehensive **family floater health insurance** policy and adds a **Critical Illness rider** to cover any unexpected health issues. She also earmarks a portion of her retirement funds for potential long-term care needs.

## 6. Estate Planning

Estate planning is crucial to ensure that your assets are distributed according to your wishes after your death. In India, many people do not pay enough attention to estate planning, but having a will and a clear distribution plan can save your family a lot of trouble.

## Key Estate Planning Elements:

- **Will:** A legally binding document that outlines how your assets should be distributed after your death.

- **Power of Attorney:** Designate someone you trust to make financial decisions on your behalf in case you become incapacitated.

- **Trusts:** For larger estates, consider setting up a trust to manage your assets and avoid complications with inheritance.

- **Nominees:** Ensure that all your financial accounts (bank, insurance, mutual funds) have updated nominees.

**Example:**

- **Rakesh**, in his early 60s, creates a **will** and designates his son as his **power of attorney**. He also sets up a **trust** for his property and other assets to ensure smooth inheritance.

*Key Takeaways:*

- **Diversify Your Income Sources:** Don't rely on just one income stream—combine pensions, investments, and rental income for financial stability.

- **Use a Sustainable Withdrawal Strategy:** Withdraw funds in a way that doesn't deplete your savings too quickly. Consider the **6 % rule** or **SWPs**.

- **Plan for Taxes:** Manage your taxes efficiently by choosing tax-friendly investments and understanding how different income sources are taxed.

- **Account for Inflation and Healthcare Costs:** Invest in growth assets, purchase adequate insurance, and review your income needs annually.

- **Estate Planning:** Ensure that your assets are distributed as per your wishes and that your loved ones are taken care of.

*"Retirement planning is not just about money; it's about ensuring a lifestyle that fits your goals and values." – Anurag*

## Chapter 8:
# Retirement Planning for Specific Goals

### Why Specific Goals Matter in Retirement Planning

While general retirement planning aims to create a broad financial foundation, specific retirement goals add clarity and purpose to your planning process. Whether you want to travel the world, fund your children's education, or ensure that you leave a legacy, retirement planning should align with your individual goals.

By breaking down your retirement needs into specific goals, you can prioritize your savings, choose the right investment options, and track your progress. This chapter will explore various specific retirement goals and how to plan for them effectively.

### 1. Planning for Travel in Retirement

One of the most common dreams in retirement is to travel—whether it's for leisure, exploration, or to visit family. However, traveling in retirement requires careful planning to cover travel costs, accommodation, and other associated expenses.

## Key Focus Areas for Travel Planning:

- **Estimate Travel Expenses:** Start by estimating how much you plan to spend on travel. This will depend on the frequency of travel, destinations, and your travel style (luxury vs. budget).

- **Set Up a Travel Fund:** Create a separate fund dedicated to your travel expenses. You can start saving for travel early in your career, or allocate a portion of your retirement corpus for this purpose.

- **Choose Flexible Travel Options:** In retirement, flexibility can be key to saving money. Consider off-season travel, budget airlines, and affordable accommodations like guesthouses, hostels, or Airbnb.

- **Use Travel Reward Programs:** Take advantage of credit cards or loyalty programs that offer travel benefits, such as discounts on flights or free hotel stays.

## Example:

- **Anuj** plans to travel to Europe and Southeast Asia every year during his retirement. He calculates that he will need ₹15 lakh annually for travel and begins saving ₹20,000 per month in a **mutual fund SIP** to build his travel fund over the next 15 years.

## 2. Retirement Planning for Children's Education

If you have children, funding their education is often a top priority. Whether your children are still young or nearing university age, it's important to plan for the rising cost of education, especially higher education.

## Key Focus Areas for Children's Education:

> **Estimate Education Costs:** Factor in inflation when estimating future education costs. For example, the cost of an engineering degree in India today might be ₹10 lakh, but inflation may make it ₹25 lakh by the time your child is ready for college.

> **Start Early with SIPs:** Invest in **SIP-based mutual funds** or **PPF** to grow your savings. The earlier you start, the more time your investments have to grow.

> **Look into Education Plans:** Some insurance companies offer **education plans** specifically designed to fund children's education, which offer life insurance coverage and a guaranteed corpus.

> **Consider Government Schemes:** Explore government schemes such as the **Sukanya Samriddhi Yojana** (for daughters) or **Pradhan Mantri Jan Dhan Yojana** for financial planning and savings.

## Example:

> **Ekta** has a young daughter and expects her to pursue a medical degree in 15 years. She estimates that it will cost ₹20 lakh, so she sets up a **mutual fund SIP** of ₹10,000 per month in an equity fund that aims for long-term growth.

## 3. Planning for Healthcare Costs

Healthcare costs rise significantly as we age, and this is one area where planning becomes extremely important. Unexpected medical expenses can quickly drain your retirement savings, so it's essential to account for these costs in your retirement plan.

## Key Focus Areas for Healthcare Planning:

- **Health Insurance Coverage:** Ensure that you have a comprehensive health insurance policy, including coverage for critical illnesses, hospitalization, and outpatient services.

- **Create a Health Fund:** In addition to insurance, set aside a separate fund specifically for medical expenses. You can use this fund to cover things that insurance doesn't, like co-pays or over-the-counter medications.

- **Plan for Long-Term Care:** As you age, there's a possibility that you may need long-term care, either in a nursing home or at home. Consider buying long-term care insurance or earmarking funds for this purpose.

- **Stay Healthy:** While not a financial aspect, maintaining good health can help reduce future medical costs. Eating a balanced diet, exercising, and staying on top of regular checkups can minimize the need for expensive treatments.

## Example:

- **Anjali** plans to allocate ₹5 lakh from her retirement corpus specifically for healthcare expenses. She buys a **comprehensive health insurance policy** and adds a **critical illness rider** to cover potential future costs.

## 4. Leaving a Legacy for Loved Ones

For many people, leaving a financial legacy for their children or grandchildren is a meaningful goal in retirement. Whether you want to provide them with an inheritance or fund a cause you care about, planning for a legacy is an important aspect of retirement.

**Key Focus Areas for Legacy Planning:**

- **Create a Will:** A will is the most basic tool for ensuring your assets are distributed as you wish. It's crucial to have one in place to avoid disputes and legal complications.

- **Establish a Trust:** If you have significant wealth, you may want to set up a **trust**. This can help manage your assets during your lifetime and ensure that your estate is handled according to your wishes after you pass away.

- **Charitable Donations:** If philanthropy is a priority for you, you can allocate a portion of your estate to charity. Many individuals set up a charitable trust or give donations directly.

- **Gifting to Heirs:** If you want to help your children or grandchildren during your lifetime, consider gifting them assets. You can do so tax-efficiently through gifting limits or by transferring assets under **Section 56** of the Income Tax Act.

**Example:**

- **Deepak** has amassed significant wealth over his lifetime and wants to leave a legacy for his children and grandchildren. He creates a **trust** to manage his estate, ensuring that the funds are distributed as he intends, and designates part of his assets for charitable causes.

## 5. Planning for Post-Retirement Income and Wealth Preservation

In addition to the specific goals mentioned above, wealth preservation in retirement is critical. Your retirement corpus needs to sustain you through your later years, so managing post-retirement income and ensuring wealth preservation should be part of your specific goal planning.

### Key Focus Areas for Income and Wealth Preservation:

- **Diversified Portfolio:** Ensure that your post-retirement portfolio includes a mix of income-producing assets like **bonds**, **fixed deposits**, **dividend-paying stocks**, and **mutual funds**.

- **Regular Portfolio Review:** Regularly review your portfolio to ensure that it aligns with your changing financial needs and that your assets are protected from inflation and market risks.

- **Systematic Withdrawal Plans (SWP):** An SWP from your mutual funds or equity investments can help you withdraw a fixed monthly income while leaving the rest of your corpus to grow.

- **Capital Preservation:** Focus on capital preservation by investing in low-risk, stable income-generating assets as you near retirement.

### Example:

- **Amyra** invests 40% of her retirement corpus in **low-risk bonds** and **fixed deposits** for stability, while the remaining 60% is invested in **equity mutual funds** with an SWP in place to generate monthly income.

**Key Takeaways:**

> - **Align Your Retirement Goals with Your Financial Plan:** Tailor your retirement plan to specific goals like travel, children's education, healthcare, or leaving a legacy.
>
> - **Start Saving Early:** The earlier you start saving for specific goals, the better. This gives you more time to accumulate the necessary funds.
>
> - **Diversify and Protect Your Wealth:** Use a diversified investment approach to manage risk while ensuring that your savings continue to grow.
>
> - **Plan for the Unexpected:** Prepare for rising healthcare costs, inflation, and other potential expenses that could arise in retirement.
>
> - **Estate and Legacy Planning:** Ensure that your assets are distributed according to your wishes and that you leave a positive impact on your loved ones or causes you care about.

*"A penny saved is a penny earned, but a penny invested in your retirement is worth a fortune later"*

*-Anurag*

## Chapter 9:
# Retirement Planning for Small Business Owners

**Understanding the Challenges of Retirement Planning for Small Business Owners**

Small business owners often face a unique set of challenges when it comes to retirement planning. Unlike salaried individuals who receive regular contributions to a retirement fund, business owners are responsible for building their own retirement savings. The business might consume a large portion of their time and attention, making it difficult to focus on long-term financial goals.

However, with the right strategies and tools, small business owners can successfully plan for retirement while continuing to run their businesses. This chapter will guide you through the essential steps to take control of your retirement planning as a small business owner.

**1. Importance of Separate Business and Personal Finances**

One of the first steps in retirement planning for small business owners is separating business finances from personal finances. It can be tempting to use the business funds for personal expenses, but this complicates retirement planning and can leave you without the savings needed for your post-retirement life.

**Steps to Separate Business and Personal Finances:**

- ➤ **Open Separate Accounts:** Ensure that your business has a separate business bank account. This helps keep track of business income, expenses, and profits.

- ➤ **Set a Salary or Draw:** Pay yourself a fixed salary or draw from the business. This ensures that you have a reliable income and can allocate funds for retirement savings.

- ➤ **Account for Business-Related Expenses:** Make sure that only business-related expenses are deducted from the business accounts, and personal expenses are handled separately.

**Example:**

- ➤ **Amit**, a small business owner, opens a dedicated business account and sets a monthly salary of ₹50,000 for himself. This allows him to contribute to a retirement plan and manage personal expenses separately.

## 2. Retirement Planning Options for Small Business Owners

As a small business owner, you don't have the benefit of a pension plan or employer-sponsored retirement fund. However, there are several retirement planning options that you can consider, tailored to self-employed individuals.

## Popular Retirement Plans for Small Business Owners:

- **Public Provident Fund (PPF):** Although not exclusive to business owners, **PPF** is a great option for building a long-term retirement corpus with tax benefits. You can invest up to ₹1.5 lakh per year, and the returns are tax-free.

- **National Pension Scheme (NPS):** NPS is another excellent option, especially for those seeking higher returns. It allows tax deductions up to ₹1.5 lakh under Section 80C and additional deductions for contributions made to the NPS.

- **Employee Provident Fund (EPF):** If you have employees, consider offering **EPF** to them, and as a business owner, you can also contribute to the EPF for yourself as a voluntary contributor.

- **Mutual Fund SIPs:** A great option for growing wealth over time. Start a **Systematic Investment Plan (SIP)** in equity or hybrid funds to grow your retirement corpus with higher returns.

- **Retirement Plans from Life Insurance Companies:** Insurance companies offer **retirement plans** designed for self-employed individuals, providing annuity-based options for regular income after retirement.

## Example:

- **Mohit,** a business owner, contributes ₹ 50,000 annually to NPS and ₹20,000 to PPF. In addition, he starts a **mutual fund SIP** of ₹ 30,000 per month to diversify his investments.

## 3. Setting Up a Business Succession Plan

A business succession plan is essential for small business owners, especially when planning for retirement. It ensures that the business will continue after the owner steps down, and can also be a key component of your retirement strategy.

**Steps for Succession Planning:**

- **Identify a Successor:** Choose someone who will take over the day-to-day operations of your business, whether it's a family member, a trusted employee, or an external buyer.

- **Develop an Exit Strategy:** Define how and when you will exit the business. This could involve selling the business, transferring it to a family member, or winding it down gradually.

- **Legal and Financial Considerations:** Ensure that the succession plan is legally sound and takes into account the business valuation, taxes, and any outstanding liabilities.

**Example:**

- **Manish** decides to hand over his family-owned hardware store to his eldest son, who has been working in the business for years. He creates a detailed succession plan, with a timeline for the transfer of ownership and clear financial goals.

## 4. Managing Cash Flow to Fund Retirement

Business owners often face fluctuating income levels. Cash flow can be unpredictable, and this affects how much can be allocated toward retirement. However, with discipline and planning, it's possible to manage cash flow effectively.

**Cash Flow Management Tips:**

- **Set Up Automatic Transfers:** Automate your retirement contributions. As soon as you receive your salary or income from the business, set up automatic transfers to your retirement accounts.

- **Build an Emergency Fund:** Ensure you have a separate emergency fund for the business and your personal expenses. This helps avoid dipping into your retirement savings during cash flow crunches.

- **Plan for Business Expenses:** Ensure that you budget properly for business-related expenses, such as payroll, rent, and supplies, without affecting your retirement savings.

**Example:**

- **Lovely,** a small business owner, sets up an automated monthly transfer of ₹30,000 to her **SIP account** and ₹10,000 to her **PPF**. She also ensures her business maintains a 6-month cash reserve for any unexpected expenses.

## 5. Building Multiple Income Streams for Retirement

Small business owners should aim to diversify their income streams to secure their retirement. Relying solely on business income can be risky, especially if the business experiences downturns.

**Ideas for Diversifying Income:**

- **Rental Income:** If you own property, consider renting it out to generate additional passive income.

- **Investing in Dividend Stocks:** Building a portfolio of dividend-paying stocks can provide a regular income stream in retirement.

- **Real Estate Investment:** Investing in commercial or residential real estate can provide a steady income through rent or capital appreciation.

- **Online Ventures:** Many business owners explore online ventures or create passive income streams through online businesses, blogs, or e-commerce.

**Example:**

- **Gaurav** owns a clothing store and invests ₹20,000 per month in a **Mutual fund's portfolio** to create an additional income stream for retirement. He also rents out a portion of his commercial property.

## 6. Tax Planning for Business Owners

Effective tax planning is crucial for small business owners. Business owners often face a higher tax burden than salaried individuals, so it's essential to structure their finances in a way that reduces taxes while maximizing retirement savings.

**Tax Planning Strategies:**

- **Claim Business Deductions:** Claim deductions for business expenses such as rent, utilities, salaries, and insurance. This will reduce taxable income.

- **Utilize Tax-Free Investment Options:** Invest in **PPF, NPS,** or **ELSS (Equity Linked Savings Schemes)** to reduce taxable income.

- **Consider Incorporating Your Business:** Incorporating your business as a private limited company can open up more tax-saving avenues and help with wealth accumulation.

**Example:**
- **Kartik** runs a graphic design studio and incorporates his business. By doing so, he can avail of lower corporate tax rates, claim more business expenses, and increase his retirement savings.

**Key Takeaways:**
- **Separate Your Business and Personal Finances:** Manage business and personal finances separately to ensure clear financial planning for retirement.

- **Explore Retirement Options:** Consider **NPS**, **PPF**, **Mutual funds**, and other retirement plans tailored for self-employed individuals.

- **Have a Succession Plan:** Plan for the future of your business by having a succession strategy in place, which will ensure business continuity.

- **Diversify Income Streams:** Aim for additional income sources outside of your business to secure your retirement.

- **Tax Planning:** Efficiently plan your taxes by leveraging business deductions, tax-free investment options, and incorporating your business.

*"Don't wait until you're tired to start planning for retirement—start now while you still have the energy to build it." – Anurag*

## Chapter 10:
# Retirement Planning for Women's

**Understanding the Retirement Planning Gap for Women**

Women often face a unique set of challenges when it comes to retirement planning. These challenges stem from factors such as longer life expectancy, wage disparities, career breaks (for marriage, motherhood, or caregiving), and, in some cases, lower financial literacy. However, women have the potential to make informed, strategic decisions that can help secure their financial future, even in the face of these obstacles.

In this chapter, we will discuss the specific hurdles women face in retirement planning, how to overcome them, and how women can plan for a secure and prosperous retirement.

**1. The Gender Pay Gap and Its Impact on Retirement Savings**

Women, on average, tend to earn less than men over their lifetimes due to wage disparities, fewer opportunities for career advancement, and career interruptions. This can have a significant impact on their ability to save for retirement. Women's lower lifetime earnings also mean smaller retirement contributions, making it harder to accumulate the wealth necessary for a comfortable retirement.

**Strategies to Overcome the Gender Pay Gap:**

> ➢ **Increase Contributions to Retirement Plans:** If you're earning less than your male counterparts, try to compensate by contributing a larger percentage of your salary to retirement savings. Make the most of **employee benefits** like **Provident Fund (PF)**, **NPS**, and **employee stock options** (ESOPs).

> ➢ **Invest in High-Growth Assets:** Since women generally live longer, they need their money to grow faster. Invest in higher-return assets such as **mutual funds**, **stocks**, and **real estate** to make up for the pay gap.

> ➢ **Focus on Career Growth:** Advocate for pay raises and seek opportunities for career advancement. Building a strong professional network can help you stay competitive in the workforce.

**Example:**

> ➢ **Payal**, despite earning a lower salary than her male colleagues, ensures that she contributes the maximum possible amount to her **NPS account** and starts a **mutual fund SIP** to increase her retirement savings. She also negotiates for better pay in her performance review.

**2. Planning for Longer Life Expectancy**

On average, women live longer than men, which means they may need to fund a longer retirement. Longer life expectancy also means that women are more likely to face the financial challenges of aging, such as healthcare costs, living alone, and the risk of outliving their savings.

**Strategies to Plan for Longer Life Expectancy:**

- ➢ **Start Saving Early:** The earlier you start saving for retirement, the more time your investments have to grow. Make it a priority to begin retirement planning as soon as possible.

- ➢ **Invest for Growth:** To build a larger retirement corpus, consider high-growth investments such as **equity mutual funds** or **stocks**. A mix of equities, bonds, and alternative assets can help balance risk and return.

- ➢ **Health Insurance and Long-Term Care:** Buy a comprehensive **health insurance policy** that covers major medical expenses and **critical illness insurance**. Additionally, look into long-term care options as you age, such as home health aides or assisted living.

**Example:**

- ➢ **Neha**, at 30, begins investing in **equity mutual funds** with a long-term horizon, contributing ₹25,000 monthly. By starting early, she ensures she has a substantial corpus by the time she retires at 60, even though she anticipates living well into her 90s.

## 3. Career Breaks for Marriage, Motherhood, or Caregiving

Many women take career breaks for reasons such as marriage, motherhood, or caregiving. These breaks can result in gaps in income, and consequently, gaps in retirement savings. This can make it difficult for women to reach the same retirement savings targets as their male counterparts.

**Strategies to Handle Career Breaks:**

- ➤ **Plan for Career Breaks in Advance:** If you're planning to take a career break, it's important to plan ahead. You should work towards building your retirement savings during your active years, so you don't miss out on contributions.

- ➤ **Use the Break for Investment Growth:** While on a career break, consider finding alternative income streams, such as **freelancing**, **consulting**, or investing in **dividend-paying stocks**.

- ➤ **Catch-Up Contributions:** If you return to work after a break, make use of catch-up contributions by increasing the percentage of your salary allocated to retirement plans.

**Example:**

- ➤ **Sonia**, after taking a 5-year break to raise her children, returns to work and makes it a priority to increase her contributions to her **PPF** and **SIP** accounts to make up for the lost years.

### 4. Overcoming the Lack of Financial Literacy

Studies show that women tend to have lower financial literacy compared to men, which can hinder their ability to make informed decisions about retirement planning. Many women are less confident in investing or managing their money, which can lead to missed opportunities.

**Strategies to Improve Financial Literacy:**

- ➤ **Educate Yourself:** Take time to educate yourself about personal finance, investing, and retirement planning. There are many online courses, books, and resources that can help you become more financially literate.

- **Seek Professional Advice:** Consider working with a **financial advisor** or **retirement planner** who can provide personalized advice and guide you in making informed decisions about your finances.
- **Join Financial Groups or Communities:** Join groups, webinars, or communities where women discuss financial topics. This can help build confidence and understanding about money management.

**Example:**
- **Amyra**, who felt uncertain about her finances, takes an online course on personal finance and investment strategies. She also consults with a **financial advisor** who helps her create a strategy for retirement savings, including investments in **Mutual funds** and **NPS**.

## 5. The Role of Spousal Support in Retirement Planning

While women should take charge of their own retirement planning, spousal support can also play an important role in creating a secure retirement. This is particularly true if one spouse has earned more or if one spouse is the primary caregiver.

**Strategies for Spousal Collaboration:**
- **Plan Together:** Retirement planning should be a joint effort. Discuss retirement goals, contributions, and savings plans with your spouse. Align your investments and ensure both of you are on track for retirement.
- **Consider Joint Investment Accounts:** If you're married, consider opening joint investment accounts such as a **joint PPF account** or **mutual fund SIPs**.

This can help consolidate savings and make the planning process smoother.

- **Understand Survivorship Planning:** Plan for what happens in case of one spouse's death. Review life insurance, **nominee designations**, and **estate planning** to ensure that both spouses' financial needs are met.

**Example:**

- **Meera** and her husband jointly set up a **PPF account** and a **mutual fund SIP**. They regularly review their retirement plans together, ensuring that both are saving adequately for a comfortable future.

## 6. The Importance of Estate Planning and Legacy Building

Women are increasingly taking the lead in managing family finances and making long-term decisions about wealth distribution. Estate planning is crucial for women, especially to ensure that their hard-earned wealth is passed on according to their wishes.

**Strategies for Effective Estate Planning:**

- **Create a Will:** Having a will ensures that your assets are distributed according to your wishes after you pass away. This is particularly important if you have dependents.

- **Establish a Trust:** A trust can be used to manage assets, especially if you have significant wealth or want to provide for your children's future education or other needs.

- **Make Use of Life Insurance:** Life insurance can be a powerful tool for ensuring financial security for your family in case of an untimely death. Consider buying adequate life insurance and naming beneficiaries.

**Example:**

**Pooja**, after building a successful career, creates a living trust and designates her children as beneficiaries. This ensures that her assets are distributed smoothly without the need for probate.

**Key Takeaways:**

- ➤ **Bridge the Pay Gap:** Increase contributions to retirement plans and focus on high-growth assets like mutual funds and stocks to overcome the gender pay gap.

- ➤ **Plan for Longevity:** Start saving early and ensure your retirement savings will last through a longer retirement period.

- ➤ **Handle Career Breaks Wisely:** Plan ahead for career breaks, and make use of catch-up contributions when you return to work.

- ➤ **Educate Yourself:** Improve financial literacy by reading books, attending courses, and seeking advice from professionals.

- ➤ **Collaborate with Your Spouse:** Plan for retirement together, considering joint investments and survivorship planning.

- ➤ **Focus on Estate Planning:** Ensure your wealth is passed on according to your wishes through wills, trusts, and life insurance.

*"The secret to a successful retirement is planning well in advance, knowing what you want, and taking the necessary steps to achieve it." – Anurag*

## Chapter 11:
# Retirement Planning for Senior Citizens

**Understanding the Financial Needs of Senior Citizens**

As people enter their retirement years, their financial needs change significantly. Senior citizens often face a fixed income, increased healthcare costs, and the need to protect their savings from inflation. Effective retirement planning during these years is essential to ensure a secure and comfortable lifestyle, without worrying about running out of money.

This chapter will discuss strategies for managing finances, maximizing income sources, and preserving wealth in the retirement phase.

**1. Reviewing Your Retirement Goals**

Once you reach retirement age, it's crucial to review your financial goals. Your goals may shift from wealth accumulation to wealth preservation, ensuring that you have enough funds for day-to-day expenses, healthcare, and leisure activities.

**Key Considerations in Reviewing Retirement Goals:**

> - **Living Expenses:** Determine your monthly and annual expenses. Make a list of essential costs, such as housing, utilities, food, and insurance, as well as

discretionary spending for hobbies, vacations, and entertainment.

- **Healthcare:** Healthcare costs tend to rise with age. Include medical insurance premiums and potential out-of-pocket costs in your retirement plan.

- **Legacy and Estate Planning:** Consider how you would like to distribute your assets, whether to family members or charitable organizations. Effective estate planning ensures your wishes are carried out.

**Example:**

- **Shivani**, a retired teacher, carefully reviews her expenses each year to ensure she's not overspending. She accounts for healthcare costs and sets aside money for travel, as she enjoys visiting new places in her retirement.

## 2. Managing Retirement Income Sources

Senior citizens often rely on a fixed income, such as pensions, annuities, or social security, in addition to any savings they have accumulated over the years. Properly managing these income sources is essential to avoid financial difficulties later on.

**Types of Retirement Income Sources:**

- **Pension:** If you have a pension plan, you can receive a regular income, but it's important to understand the payment schedule, tax implications, and whether it will cover your living expenses.

- **Annuities:** Fixed annuities can provide a steady stream of income throughout retirement. Consider whether an annuity is a good option for you, especially if you're concerned about outliving your savings.

- **Public Provident Fund (PPF) and Fixed Deposits (FDs):** While PPF and FDs are long-term savings tools, they can also be useful for senior citizens seeking stable, risk-free returns. Interest from these instruments can provide a reliable source of income.
- **Dividend Stocks and Mutual Funds:** If you have a stock portfolio or investments in mutual funds, you may receive regular dividends. Be sure to balance the risk of the investments with the need for stable income.
- **Rental Income:** If you own property, renting it out can provide consistent income.

**Example:**

- **Rajesh**, a retiree, receives a monthly pension of ₹30,000 and has invested in **FDs** and **dividend-paying stocks**, providing him with an additional ₹15,000 each month. This combined income ensures that his basic living expenses are met.

## 3. Managing Healthcare Costs in Retirement

Healthcare expenses increase significantly with age. In addition to regular checkups and medication, there is always the possibility of unexpected medical issues that require substantial financial resources. Therefore, it's essential to plan for healthcare costs in retirement.

**Strategies to Manage Healthcare Costs:**

- **Health Insurance:** Senior citizens should invest in comprehensive health insurance policies that cover hospital bills, surgeries, and critical illnesses. Look for policies that offer **cashless hospitalization** and coverage for specific senior citizen needs.

➢ **Critical Illness Insurance:** This can help cover the costs of major illnesses, including cancer, heart disease, or stroke, which can be financially devastating.

➢ **Government Schemes and Benefits:** Explore government health schemes specifically designed for senior citizens. In India, programs such as **Ayushman Bharat** provide medical insurance to low-income seniors.

**Example:**

➢ **Vinod**, a senior citizen, takes out a **senior citizen health insurance policy** that covers hospital bills and critical illnesses. He also checks for coverage under **Ayushman Bharat** to ensure he's protected from unexpected medical expenses.

## 4. Minimizing Tax Burden in Retirement

In retirement, income taxes can take a significant portion of your monthly income. Senior citizens must be mindful of their tax liabilities and take steps to minimize taxes on their retirement income.

**Tax Planning Strategies:**

➢ **Tax-Free Investment Options:** Investments in **PPF, NPS**, and **tax-free bonds** can provide tax relief. Be sure to include these in your retirement portfolio.

➢ **Tax-Saving Instruments:** Take advantage of tax-saving instruments like **Senior Citizens Savings Scheme (SCSS)**, which offers tax benefits and a higher interest rate for individuals aged 60 and above.

- **Capital Gains Tax:** If you have investments in stocks, real estate, or mutual funds, be aware of the capital gains tax implications when you sell assets. Holding investments for the long term can reduce capital gains tax.

- **Income Tax Exemption for Seniors:** Senior citizens can claim higher exemptions under the Income Tax Act. Familiarize yourself with these exemptions and make the most of them.

**Example:**

- **Sarita**, a retired government employee, invests in **SCSS** and **NPS** to avail tax exemptions. By carefully managing her income and expenses, she keeps her tax liabilities low.

## 5. Protecting Your Wealth and Assets

As a senior citizen, preserving your wealth is just as important as accumulating it. At this stage, the focus should be on protecting your assets from inflation, market volatility, and any unforeseen financial risks.

**Strategies to Protect Wealth:**

- **Diversify Investments:** Diversification is key to protecting your wealth. Ensure that your portfolio includes a mix of fixed-income investments (such as FDs and PPF), equities, and other assets like gold or real estate.

- **Downsize Your Property:** If you no longer need a large home, consider downsizing to a smaller property. This can free up cash that can be invested or used for other purposes.

- **Avoid Risky Investments:** Avoid speculative investments or high-risk stocks that could jeopardize your wealth. Stick to low-risk, stable investments like **bonds**, **FDs**, and **NPS**.

- **Estate Planning:** Ensure you have a will in place that clearly outlines how your assets will be distributed to your heirs. This helps avoid family disputes and ensures your wealth is passed on according to your wishes.

**Example:**

- **Niranjan**, a retired engineer, sells his large house and buys a smaller, more affordable apartment. The proceeds from the sale are invested in Mutual Funds, Gold **bonds** and **NPS**, ensuring long-term security and preservation of his wealth.

## 6. Social and Emotional Wellbeing in Retirement

Retirement is not just about financial security; it's also about maintaining a fulfilling and active lifestyle. Senior citizens often face emotional challenges such as loneliness, loss of purpose, and health issues. It's important to engage in activities that promote emotional and social wellbeing.

**Strategies for Maintaining Social and Emotional Wellbeing:**

- **Stay Active:** Engage in regular physical activity, such as walking, yoga, or swimming, to stay healthy. Physical activity can also boost mood and reduce stress.

- **Volunteer or Take Up Hobbies:** Volunteering for social causes or pursuing hobbies like painting, gardening, or learning new skills can provide a sense of purpose and fulfilment.

- **Stay Connected:** Stay in touch with friends, family, and community members. Join clubs or senior citizen groups to maintain social connections and prevent isolation.

**Example:**

- **Kavita**, a retired teacher, joins a local **book club** and takes up **painting classes**. She also volunteers at a local charity, which gives her a sense of purpose and keeps her emotionally fulfilled.

**Key Takeaways:**

- **Review Retirement Goals:** Regularly assess your retirement goals and adjust your budget and lifestyle to match your income.

- **Maximize Income Sources:** Make the most of available income sources such as pensions, annuities, and dividend income to meet your financial needs.

- **Plan for Healthcare Costs:** Invest in health insurance and critical illness cover to protect against rising medical costs.

- **Minimize Taxes:** Use tax-saving instruments and take advantage of exemptions available to senior citizens to minimize your tax burden.

- **Protect Your Wealth:** Diversify investments and focus on low-risk, stable assets to preserve wealth during retirement.

- **Promote Emotional Wellbeing:** Engage in activities that keep you active, socially connected, and emotionally fulfilled.

*"Failing to plan for retirement is like sailing without a map you may reach your destination, but the journey will be uncertain." – Anurag*

## Chapter 12:
# Retirement Planning for Couples

## The Importance of Joint Retirement Planning

Retirement planning for couples requires collaboration, transparency, and compromise. A successful retirement plan considers both partners' individual goals, life stages, and financial habits. When both partners work together to plan for the future, they can align their efforts toward achieving a comfortable, financially secure retirement.

This chapter will explore the steps couples can take to build a retirement plan that works for both partners, ensuring a smooth transition into retirement.

## 1. Open Communication and Setting Shared Retirement Goals

The foundation of a successful retirement plan for couples is open and honest communication. Both partners need to be clear about their expectations, dreams, and concerns about retirement.

### Key Elements of Setting Shared Retirement Goals:

- **Retirement Age:** Agree on the age at which both partners want to retire. This will determine the time horizon for saving and investing.

- **Lifestyle Expectations:** Discuss what kind of lifestyle you both envision in retirement. Do you want to travel frequently, move to a different city or country, or enjoy a quiet life at home?

- **Health and Care Needs:** Consider your potential healthcare needs as you age. It's important to plan for health insurance, long-term care, and medical expenses.

- **Financial Independence:** Ensure that both partners are working toward financial independence, with enough income to support your desired lifestyle.

**Example:**

- **Barun and Mala** decide they want to retire at 60 and travel the world. They agree on setting up a joint savings account where both contribute a fixed percentage of their income every month toward their travel fund and retirement savings.

## 2. Reviewing and Combining Finances

When it comes to retirement planning, it's important to assess your individual financial situations and combine resources where possible. This includes understanding each partner's income, expenses, assets, and liabilities, as well as any retirement accounts or pension plans.

**Steps for Reviewing and Combining Finances:**

- **Debt Management:** Pay off any high-interest debts before retirement. This will reduce your financial burden in your later years.

- **Asset Allocation:** Consider whether both partners' assets are aligned with your retirement goals. Jointly manage investments to ensure a balanced portfolio that includes **Equity mutual funds**, **PPF**, **fixed deposits**, and other stable, income-generating assets.

- **Retirement Accounts:** Consolidate pension plans, **NPS**, and **employee provident fund (EPF)** accounts if possible. Ensure both partners are maximizing contributions to retirement accounts.

- **Review Expenses:** Re-evaluate household expenses, such as mortgage payments or children's education costs, to determine what can be reduced or eliminated.

**Example:**

- **Vikram and Anjali** decide to review their individual investment portfolios and consolidate them into a joint investment account. They set up **SIP** (Systematic Investment Plans) for their mutual fund investments and allocate a portion of their monthly income to both **NPS** and **PPF** accounts.

## 3. Balancing Retirement Contributions and Adjusting Savings Plans

One common issue couple face in retirement planning is the unequal contribution to retirement savings. This could happen if one partner earns more or has a higher retirement plan. Balancing contributions and adjusting plans accordingly is essential for both partners to have a similar level of financial security.

**Steps for Balancing Contributions:**

- **Equalize Contributions:** Even if one partner earns more, try to contribute equally in terms of percentage of income toward retirement savings.

- **Review Joint Investment Strategies:** Allocate investments based on your risk tolerance, time horizon, and goals. Ensure you both have the opportunity to take advantage of tax-saving investment options like **NPS, SCSS**, or **PPF**.

> **Catch-Up Contributions:** If one partner had to take a career break or was unable to contribute to retirement savings for some reason, they can make additional contributions to catch up.

**Example:**

> **Deepak** earns a higher salary than **Priya**, but they agree to contribute 15% of their individual monthly income into their **mutual fund SIPs** and retirement accounts. **Priya** also increases her contribution slightly to make up for the years she was on maternity leave.

## 4. Creating a Contingency Fund for Emergencies

Couples should plan for unexpected events such as health issues, job loss, or other emergencies that may arise in the years leading up to or during retirement. A contingency fund ensures that unexpected expenses don't derail your long-term retirement plans.

### Steps to Create a Contingency Fund:

> **Start an Emergency Fund:** Aim to have at least 6–12 months' worth of living expenses in a liquid, easily accessible account. This fund can be used to cover sudden medical expenses or urgent financial needs.

> **Separate Accounts for Joint and Personal Expenses:** Keep a joint emergency fund, but also have personal funds for unexpected expenses or personal goals.

**Example:**

- **Sandeep and Amrita** create a **joint emergency fund** of ₹ 10 lakhs, which they keep in a liquid savings account. They also have personal emergency funds, which they can dip into if needed.

## 5. Managing Healthcare and Long-Term Care Expenses Together

Healthcare costs tend to rise with age, and couples need to plan together for medical expenses, especially as they grow older. Senior citizens may face large medical bills, so it's essential to have sufficient health insurance coverage.

**Steps for Managing Healthcare Costs:**

- **Health Insurance Plans:** Look for health insurance plans that provide comprehensive coverage for both partners. Ensure your plans cover hospitalization, outpatient care, and critical illnesses.

- **Critical Illness Insurance:** Both partners should consider purchasing critical illness insurance that will cover major diseases like cancer, stroke, or heart conditions.

- **Long-Term Care:** As you age, you may require long-term care, such as home health aides or assisted living. Plan for this by setting aside funds or purchasing long-term care insurance.

**Example:**

- **Vijay and Rekha** purchase a **comprehensive health insurance plan** that covers both hospitalization and medical expenses for each of them. They also set aside an additional ₹ 20,000 per month for potential long-term care needs.

## 6. Planning for Legacy and Estate Distribution

Estate planning is an important part of retirement planning for couples. Both partners should clearly communicate how they want their assets distributed and take the necessary steps to create a will, set up a trust, or designate beneficiaries.

**Steps for Estate Planning:**

- ➢ **Create a Will:** A will ensures that your assets are distributed according to your wishes. Both partners should create their individual wills, but also discuss any shared assets and joint accounts.

- ➢ **Set Up a Trust:** A trust can be useful for couples who want to leave a legacy for their children or grandchildren while avoiding the complexities of probate.

- ➢ **Nominee Designations:** Ensure that your retirement accounts, life insurance policies, and other financial assets have clear nominee designations to streamline the transfer of assets upon death.

**Example:**

- ➢ **Kiran and Praveen** create a **joint will** outlining how they want to divide their assets, including properties and investments. They set up a **living trust** for their children's education fund and designate beneficiaries for their **life insurance policies**.

## 7. Transitioning to Retirement Together

As you approach retirement, it's important to transition gradually to ensure that you and your partner are both financially and emotionally prepared for the changes.

## Steps for a Smooth Transition:

- ➤ **Test Your Retirement Budget:** Start living on your projected retirement income a few years before retirement to ensure you can manage your finances effectively without the stress of sudden lifestyle changes.

- ➤ **Practice Retirement Activities:** Use your free time before retirement to explore hobbies, travel, or volunteer together. This helps both partners adjust to the idea of retirement and create new shared goals.

- ➤ **Discuss Future Plans:** Keep the lines of communication open about what both partners want to do in retirement. This could involve traveling, starting a business, or giving back to the community.

## Example:

- ➤ **Amit and Sonai** begin by reducing their working hours a few years before retirement, allowing them to test their retirement budget. They spend more time traveling together and discuss how they will continue to be active in retirement.

## Key Takeaways:

- ➤ **Communication is the Key:** Open discussions about your retirement goals, finances, and future plans are essential for a successful retirement.

- ➤ **Balance Contributions:** Work together to balance retirement contributions and adjust savings plans based on income and life stages.

- ➤ **Healthcare and Long-Term Care:** Plan for rising healthcare and long-term care costs, ensuring both partners are covered.

- ➤ **Estate Planning:** Create wills, trusts, and designate beneficiaries to ensure that your wealth is passed on according to your wishes.
- ➤ **Smooth Transition to Retirement:** Transition gradually into retirement, testing your budget and discussing shared goals and activities for this new phase of life.

*"If you don't make a plan for your future, someone else will do it for you—and they may not have your best interests at heart." – Anurag*

## Chapter 13:
# Retirement Planning for Self-Employed Individuals & Entrepreneur's.

**The Challenges of Retirement Planning for Self-Employed People & Entrepreneurs.**

Unlike salaried employees, self-employed individuals do not have the benefit of employer-sponsored retirement plans, such as SIP, **EPF** (Employee Provident Fund), **Gratuity**, or **pension schemes**. This makes it essential for them to take proactive steps in creating their own retirement plans. The absence of regular employer contributions means self-employed individuals must manage their finances independently and consistently save for the future.

This chapter will explore the strategies that self-employed individuals can adopt to ensure a financially secure and comfortable retirement.

### 1. Understanding the Importance of Self-Funded Retirement

Self-employed individuals need to understand the importance of funding their own retirement. Without the support of a corporate pension plan, your retirement savings depend entirely on your own efforts.

## Why Self-Funded Retirement is Essential:

- **No Employer Contribution:** Unlike salaried employees, self-employed individuals must fund both their own contributions to retirement plans.

- **Uncertain Income:** The income of a self-employed individual can fluctuate, making it challenging to save consistently. However, this should not deter you from prioritizing retirement savings.

- **Greater Control:** The upside is that self-employed individuals have greater control over how and when they contribute to their retirement funds, allowing for flexibility.

## Example:

- **Akshat** runs a small graphic design business. His income varies from month to month, but he makes it a point to set aside 30% of his monthly earnings into a dedicated retirement savings account.

## 2. Creating a Retirement Savings Strategy

Self-employed individuals need to develop a clear retirement savings strategy, which involves setting up personal retirement accounts, automating savings, and sticking to a disciplined approach.

## Key Elements of a Retirement Savings Strategy:

- **Set Retirement Goals:** Clearly define your retirement age, lifestyle, and income requirements. This will guide how much you need to save.

- **Assess Current Savings and Investments:** Take stock of your current savings, investment portfolio, and any existing retirement contributions to evaluate if you are on track.

- **Save Regularly, Even in Low-Income Months:** Develop a plan to save a percentage of your income every month, even if it's a smaller amount during lean months.

- **Invest Wisely:** Invest in a diversified portfolio that includes long-term growth assets, such as **equity mutual funds**, **stocks**, and **bonds**.

**Example:**

- **Amyra**, a freelance writer, has set up a **Systematic Investment Plan (SIP)** for ₹25,000 per month in equity mutual funds and also invests in **PPF** to ensure tax savings and growth.

### 3. Choosing the Right Retirement Accounts

As a self-employed individual, you don't have the benefit of employer-sponsored retirement plans. However, there are several tax-advantageous accounts that you can contribute to, helping you grow your retirement savings while reducing tax liability.

**Retirement Accounts to Consider:**

- **National Pension Scheme (NPS):** NPS offers an excellent retirement savings option with tax benefits and a low-cost investment structure. As a self-employed person, you can contribute voluntarily to NPS, receiving tax deductions under Section 80C and 80CCD.

- **Public Provident Fund (PPF):** PPF is a government-backed savings scheme that provides tax-free returns and a guaranteed interest rate. It's ideal for long-term savings and retirement planning.

- **Sukanya Samriddhi Yojana (if applicable):** If you have a daughter, this government scheme offers attractive interest rates and tax-saving benefits.

- **Fixed Deposits (FDs):** While FDs offer lower returns, they are a safe option for parking funds for short-term financial goals and a part of retirement savings.

- **Employee Provident Fund (EPF) for Self-Employed:** You can voluntarily contribute to EPF as a self-employed individual under the **EPF Voluntary Contribution Scheme**.

**Example:**

- **Rakesh**, a self-employed consultant, contributes ₹12,000 monthly to his **NPS** account. He also invests ₹6,000 per month in a **PPF** account to benefit from tax deductions and build a steady retirement corpus.

## 4. Diversifying Your Investments for a Stable Retirement Fund

Self-employed individuals need to focus on growing their retirement savings through investments that offer both growth potential and stability. A diversified investment strategy that balances risk and return is essential for long-term success.

### Investment Options to Consider:

- **Equity Mutual Funds:** These provide high growth potential but come with higher risk. Investing in diversified equity mutual funds can help you grow your wealth.

- **Debt Funds:** These provide steady returns with lower risk compared to equities. Debt funds like **bond mutual funds** can balance the portfolio.

- **Stocks:** If you're comfortable with higher risk, individual stocks can offer great returns. However, they should be a smaller portion of your retirement portfolio.

- **Gold:** Investing in **gold** through **Sovereign Gold Bonds (SGBs)** or **gold ETFs** can provide a hedge against inflation and add diversification to your portfolio.

- **Real Estate:** If your capital allows, consider investing in rental properties for passive income in retirement.

**Example:**

- **Ravi**, a self-employed entrepreneur, has invested in a combination of **equity mutual funds**, **gold ETFs**, and **real estate**. This diversified portfolio helps him manage risk while growing his retirement fund.

## 5. Managing Cash Flow and Creating a Contingency Fund

A common challenge for self-employed individuals is managing irregular income. During lean months, it's essential to ensure that you can still contribute to your retirement savings. One way to handle this is by creating a contingency fund.

**Strategies for Managing Cash Flow:**

- **Separate Savings for Retirement:** Create a separate account specifically for retirement savings so you don't dip into it for day-to-day expenses.

- ➢ **Build an Emergency Fund:** This fund should cover 6-12 months of living expenses and be easily accessible. Having a strong emergency fund allows you to continue your retirement contributions even during tough months.
- ➢ **Adjust Contributions Based on Income:** In months with lower income, consider reducing your retirement contributions temporarily rather than skipping them altogether.

**Example:**
- ➢ **Akshat**, a self-employed photographer, ensures that he sets aside 15% of his income for retirement savings. During slow seasons, he relies on his emergency fund to cover living expenses and continues contributing to his retirement accounts.

## 6. Planning for Taxes and Maximizing Tax Benefits

Self-employed individuals can take advantage of several tax-saving instruments to reduce their taxable income and grow their retirement savings efficiently. Understanding tax laws and utilizing these benefits is crucial for maximizing retirement savings.

**Key Tax Benefits:**
- ➢ **NPS Contributions:** Contributions to the **NPS** are eligible for tax deductions under Section 80C and 80CCD (1) up to ₹2 lakh. This can significantly reduce your taxable income.
- ➢ **PPF Contributions:** Contributions to **PPF** also qualify for tax deductions under Section 80C up to ₹1.5 lakh. The interest earned and maturity proceeds are tax-free.

➢ **Tax-Free Interest from FDs and Bonds:** Some fixed-income products, such as **tax-free bonds**, provide tax-free interest, which can be beneficial for self-employed individuals looking to reduce their tax burden.

**Example:**

➢ **Ajay**, a self-employed architect, contributes ₹1.5 lakh annually to his **NPS** and **PPF** accounts, using the tax benefits to reduce his taxable income. He also invests in **tax-free bonds** to ensure that his post-tax returns are maximized.

### 7. Protecting Your Retirement Savings with Insurance

Self-employed individuals often don't have the luxury of employer-sponsored health and life insurance. Protecting your income and assets through appropriate insurance policies is essential for safeguarding your retirement plan.

**Insurance Coverage to Consider:**

➢ **Life Insurance:** A good life insurance policy ensures that your family is financially protected in case something happens to you before retirement.

➢ **Health Insurance:** Medical emergencies can derail your retirement savings if you don't have adequate coverage. Ensure you have a comprehensive health insurance policy that covers hospitalization and critical illnesses.

➢ **Disability Insurance:** Consider disability insurance to replace lost income in case of illness or injury that prevents you from working.

**Example:**
- **Ankit**, a freelance software developer, has both **life insurance** and **health insurance** policies in place. He also invests in **critical illness coverage** to ensure his family is protected in case of unexpected events.

**Key Takeaways:**
- **Start Saving Early:** Begin saving and investing for retirement as soon as possible to take advantage of compounding.

- **Diversify Investments:** Build a diversified portfolio that includes a mix of growth-oriented and stable investments to manage risk.

- **Utilize Tax Benefits:** Take advantage of tax-saving instruments like **NPS**, **PPF**, and **tax-free bonds** to reduce your taxable income.

- **Protect Your Income:** Invest in life, health, and disability insurance to safeguard your retirement savings and income.

*"The time to start planning for retirement is when you begin your career, not when you are ready to retire."*
*– Anurag*

## Chapter 14:
# Retirement Planning for High Net-Worth Individuals (HNWI)

**Introduction: Understanding the HNWI Retirement Landscape**

High net-worth individuals (HNWIs) have accumulated significant wealth and typically have more complex financial situations. They often own multiple assets, such as real estate, stocks, business interests, and other high-value investments. With their financial position comes the need for sophisticated retirement planning that considers tax efficiency, wealth preservation, legacy planning, and income diversification.

This chapter will explore tailored retirement strategies for HNWIs, helping them preserve and grow their wealth while ensuring a financially secure and comfortable retirement.

**1. The Unique Retirement Needs of HNWIs**

HNWIs face unique retirement challenges and opportunities compared to the general population. While they may have more assets, their concerns typically revolve around how to manage and protect their wealth while ensuring that they can maintain their desired lifestyle throughout retirement.

## Key Considerations for HNWIs:

- ➢ **Wealth Preservation:** Ensuring that wealth is protected from market volatility, inflation, and taxes.

- ➢ **Tax Efficiency:** High net-worth individuals often face significant tax burdens, so finding ways to minimize taxes while growing wealth is essential.

- ➢ **Legacy Planning:** Many HNWIs want to ensure that their wealth is passed on to future generations in a tax-efficient manner, making estate planning a priority.

- ➢ **Diversified Income Streams:** Diversifying income sources to reduce dependency on a single asset class or investment.

## Example:

- ➢ **Anurag and Monika**, a couple with a substantial investment portfolio, are concerned about how to protect their wealth during retirement. They seek strategies to minimize taxes, maximize income, and pass on their wealth to their children.

## 2. Maximizing Tax Efficiency

Tax efficiency is a top priority for HNWIs. By utilizing tax-efficient investment strategies, they can reduce their taxable income, increase their retirement savings, and retain more of their wealth.

## Tax-Efficient Strategies for HNWIs:

- ➢ **Capital Gains Planning:** Long-term capital gains are typically taxed at a lower rate than short-term gains. HNWIs should focus on investing in assets that generate long-term capital gains, such as real estate, stocks, and equity mutual funds.

- ➤ **Income Splitting:** HNWIs can explore ways to split income between family members in lower tax brackets to reduce the overall family tax burden. This can be done through gifting assets or setting up family trusts.

- ➤ **Tax-Advantaged Accounts:** Contributing to tax-advantaged accounts such as **NPS** (National Pension System) and **PPF** can provide immediate tax deductions and help reduce taxable income.

- ➤ **Structured Products:** HNWIs can explore structured products and tax-efficient investment vehicles, such as tax-free bonds, to generate interest income without incurring taxes.

**Example:**
- ➤ **Raghav**, an entrepreneur, invests in **long-term equity mutual funds** and holds onto real estate investments for long periods to take advantage of long-term capital gains tax benefits. Additionally, he sets up a **family trust** to allocate income to his children, reducing the overall tax burden.

## 3. Diversifying Investment Assets for Long-Term Growth

HNWIs should focus on creating a diversified investment portfolio to reduce risk and ensure stable, long-term growth. Diversification helps balance the impact of market fluctuations on retirement income and provides a safety net against economic downturns.

### Types of Assets to Include in a Diversified Portfolio:

- ➤ **Equities and Mutual Funds:** High-growth investments such as stocks and equity mutual funds should form a significant portion of the portfolio.

These investments provide potential for capital appreciation.

➢ **Fixed Income Instruments:** Bonds, **corporate deposits**, and **tax-free bonds** help stabilize the portfolio by providing predictable income streams.

➢ **Alternative Investments:** HNWIs can explore alternative investments such as private equity, hedge funds, and **real estate**. These assets are less correlated with stock markets and can provide higher returns.

➢ **International Exposure:** Investing in international markets provides geographical diversification and protection against domestic economic risks.

**Example:**

➢ **Kiran**, an HNWI, has a diversified portfolio comprising 40% **equity mutual funds**, 30% **real estate**, 20% **bonds**, and 10% in international stocks. This mix allows her to achieve growth while minimizing risks.

## 4. Wealth Preservation Through Estate Planning

Estate planning is crucial for HNWIs, as it helps protect wealth from potential liabilities, taxes, and unforeseen events. A comprehensive estate plan ensures that assets are passed on according to the individual's wishes while minimizing estate taxes.

### Key Components of Estate Planning:

➢ **Creating a Will:** A will allows you to specify how your assets should be distributed after your passing. This is particularly important for HNWIs with multiple assets, such as business interests, real estate, and financial investments.

- **Setting Up Trusts:** Family trusts can help protect assets from estate taxes and allow wealth to be passed on to heirs in a controlled manner. HNWIs often use **revocable** or **irrevocable trusts** to manage the distribution of their wealth.

- **Life Insurance:** Life insurance can provide liquidity for estate taxes or provide financial security to dependents. HNWIs may also use life insurance to fund a trust or ensure that beneficiaries receive a tax-free death benefit.

- **Gifting Strategy:** HNWIs often use gifting strategies to transfer wealth to their heirs while taking advantage of gift tax exemptions and reducing the size of their estate.

**Example:**

- **Sanjay**, a high-net-worth business owner, creates a **revocable trust** to transfer his business assets to his children while minimizing estate taxes. He also purchases a **life insurance policy** to cover any potential estate taxes and ensure a smooth transfer of wealth.

## 5. Considering Health and Long-Term Care Costs

As individuals approach retirement, healthcare costs become an increasingly important concern. For HNWIs, healthcare costs can be a significant burden, especially if they require long-term care.

**Health and Long-Term Care Planning:**

- **Health Insurance:** While most HNWIs have private health insurance, it's essential to review policies periodically to ensure comprehensive coverage, especially for age-related conditions.

- ➢ **Critical Illness Coverage:** HNWIs may consider purchasing **critical illness insurance** to provide a lump sum in the event of a serious illness, which can help cover medical expenses without affecting retirement savings.

- ➢ **Long-Term Care Insurance:** Long-term care insurance can provide coverage for nursing home care or home healthcare, which is increasingly important as individuals age.

- ➢ **Health Savings Accounts (HSAs):** HNWIs may use **HSAs** to save for medical expenses in a tax-efficient manner, allowing funds to grow over time and be used for healthcare costs in retirement.

**Example:**

- ➢ **Anjali**, a high-net-worth individual, invests in **critical illness insurance** and also sets up a **health savings account (HSA)** to cover potential healthcare expenses in retirement, ensuring that she won't need to dip into her retirement corpus for medical costs.

## 6. Maintaining a Sustainable Lifestyle in Retirement

HNWIs often have a high standard of living, and maintaining that lifestyle in retirement requires careful planning. Retirement planning for HNWIs isn't just about wealth preservation—it's about ensuring that they can enjoy the same lifestyle during retirement as they did during their working years.

**Strategies to Maintain a Sustainable Lifestyle:**

- ➢ **Withdrawal Strategy:** Develop a sustainable withdrawal strategy to ensure that your retirement savings last throughout your retirement. Many

HNWIs use the **6% rule**, which suggests withdrawing **6%** of your retirement portfolio each year to ensure long-term sustainability.

- **Income-Producing Assets:** Invest in assets that generate reliable income, such as dividend-paying stocks, rental properties, or fixed-income instruments. These assets provide a steady income stream during retirement.

- **Monitor and Adjust:** Regularly review your retirement plan to adjust for changes in your lifestyle, inflation, and unexpected events. Ensuring your portfolio is rebalanced periodically is essential to maintaining financial security.

**Example:**

- **Rajesh**, an HNWI, withdraws 6% annually from his investment portfolio, including **dividend stocks** and **real estate income**, ensuring a steady income stream while maintaining his lifestyle.

## 7. Creating a Legacy: Passing Wealth to Future Generations

For many HNWIs, retirement planning is not just about their own financial security; it's also about leaving a legacy for future generations. Effective legacy planning ensures that wealth is passed down according to your wishes, with minimal tax implications.

**Legacy Planning Strategies:**

- **Trusts for Wealth Transfer:** Use family trusts to transfer wealth to future generations while minimizing taxes and controlling how and when beneficiaries receive their inheritance.

- **Charitable Giving:** Some HNWIs choose to include charitable giving in their estate plan. By donating to charity through a **donor-advised fund** or charitable trust, they can reduce estate taxes while making a positive impact.

- **Family Governance:** Create a governance structure to involve future generations in managing wealth, ensuring that they are educated about managing and preserving the wealth you've built.

**Example:**

- **Nisha**, an HNWI, sets up a **charitable trust** to donate a portion of her wealth while providing significant tax benefits. She also involves her children in managing the family wealth, ensuring they are prepared to continue her legacy.

**Key Takeaways:**

- **Tax Efficiency:** Focus on minimizing taxes through capital gains planning, income splitting, and using tax-advantaged accounts.

- **Diversification:** Build a diversified portfolio that includes equities, fixed income, alternative investments, and international assets.

- **Wealth Preservation:** Use trusts, life insurance, and estate planning strategies to protect and pass on wealth efficiently.

- **Healthcare Planning:** Plan for healthcare and long-term care costs with insurance and savings accounts to avoid depleting retirement funds.

> **Legacy Planning:** Create a legacy plan that ensures wealth is passed on according to your wishes while minimizing tax implications.

*"Retirement planning is not just about money—it's about securing the time, freedom, and opportunities to live the life you've always dreamed of."* – *Anurag*

## Chapter 15:
# Retirement Planning for Different Stages of Life

**Introduction: The Importance of Age-Based Retirement Planning**

The earlier you start planning for retirement, the better positioned you'll be to accumulate wealth over time. However, as you progress through different life stages, your approach to retirement planning will need to shift based on your current financial situation, goals, and responsibilities.

This chapter will guide you through how retirement planning should look at each major stage of life, from your early career years to your pre-retirement years.

**1. Retirement Planning in Your 20s: The Foundation Years**

Your 20s are the perfect time to lay the foundation for a financially secure retirement. At this age, you may not have significant responsibilities like dependents or a mortgage, making it an ideal time to start saving and investing for the future.

**Key Steps to Take in Your 20s:**

> ➢ **Start Early:** Time is your greatest ally when it comes to retirement planning. The sooner you start

investing, the more your money will grow through compounding.

- **Set Financial Goals:** Determine how much money you'll need in retirement. Even if it's a rough estimate, having a target will help you focus your savings and investment efforts.

- **Automate Savings:** Set up **Systematic Investment Plans (SIPs)** for mutual funds or direct debits to a **PPF** account. Automating your savings helps ensure consistency.

- **Build a Financial Safety Net:** Start creating an emergency fund to cover at least 6 months of living expenses. This will give you financial security in case of unexpected events.

**Example:**

- **Piyush,** a 25-year-old marketing professional, invests ₹10,000 every month in a diversified equity mutual fund through SIPs. By the time he reaches 45, this early habit of saving will accumulate significantly.

## 2. Retirement Planning in Your 30s: Building Wealth and Protecting It

In your 30s, your financial situation should begin to stabilize. You may have a higher earning potential, but you may also have added responsibilities, such as buying a home or starting a family. Balancing saving for retirement with these other financial obligations is key.

**Key Steps to Take in Your 30s:**

- **Increase Savings Rate:** As your income increases, try to save a higher percentage of your earnings. Aim to save 20% or more of your income towards retirement.

- **Invest in Growth Assets:** At this stage, your investment strategy should include higher-risk, higher-return options such as **equity mutual funds** and **stocks**. These investments will give you higher returns over the long term.

- **Review Insurance Needs:** Life insurance, health insurance, and critical illness insurance become more important in your 30s, especially if you have dependents.

- **Consider Real Estate Investments:** If your finances allow, consider investing in real estate for long-term wealth building.

**Example:**

- **Priya**, at age 33, has increased her monthly SIP contribution to ₹15,000 in a mix of equity and hybrid funds. She's also purchased a **term life insurance policy** to protect her family and a **health insurance policy** for herself and her spouse.

## 3. Retirement Planning in Your 40s: Maximizing Contributions

Your 40s are a critical decade for retirement planning. By this stage, you're likely to have accumulated some savings, but you still have time to build a solid retirement corpus. Now is the time to assess your financial progress and make sure you're on track.

**Key Steps to Take in Your 40s:**

- **Focus on Maximizing Contributions:** This is the time to maximize your contributions to retirement accounts like **NPS**, **EPF**, and **PPF**. If you haven't already, consider increasing your SIPs or making lump sum investments.

- ➤ **Reduce Debt:** Try to pay off high-interest debt, such as credit card balances or personal loans, to free up more income for retirement savings.

- ➤ **Rebalance Your Portfolio:** Your asset allocation should start to become more conservative as you approach your 50s. Rebalance your portfolio to include more stable investments, such as **debt funds**, **bonds**, or **gold**.

- ➤ **Ensure Comprehensive Insurance Coverage:** You should now have adequate life, health, and critical illness insurance in place, especially if you have dependents.

**Example:**

- **Sunil**, 44 years old, works as an entrepreneur. He has a mix of **NPS**, **SIP investments**, and **Gold ETFs**. He also bought a **critical illness plan** to protect his savings in case of health emergencies. His aim is to maximize his **NPS contributions** in the coming years to avail of tax benefits and ensure a steady income post-retirement.

## 4. Retirement Planning in Your 50s: Preparing for Retirement

In your 50s, retirement may feel much closer, and it's time to fine-tune your retirement strategy. Your focus should now be on consolidating your wealth and ensuring that it will last throughout your retirement years.

**Key Steps to Take in Your 50s:**

- **Review Your Retirement Goals:** Revisit your retirement goals and make any necessary adjustments based on your current financial situation. Calculate how much you need to save each month to meet your retirement goals.

- **Increase Contributions to Safe Investments:** By this stage, your retirement corpus should be well on its way. Now, it's time to focus on safe, stable investments like **PPF, Senior Citizens' Savings Scheme (SCSS)**, and **bonds**.

- **Diversify Income Streams:** Consider diversifying your income sources. If possible, set up a **pension plan** through **NPS** or invest in **rental properties** to create a passive income stream for retirement.

- **Prepare for Health Care Costs:** Medical expenses rise as you age. Make sure you have a solid **health insurance** policy and an emergency fund to cover potential medical emergencies.

**Example:**

- **Asha**, 54 years old, is focused on maximizing her **SCSS** contributions. She has reduced her exposure to equities and is now investing in more stable **debt funds** and **fixed deposits** to ensure the safety of her corpus. She also added a **critical illness policy** to safeguard against potential medical costs in retirement.

## 5. Retirement Planning in Your 60s: Securing Your Future

By the time you reach your 60s, retirement may already be a reality. If you haven't yet retired, your focus will be on ensuring that your retirement income will be sufficient to maintain your lifestyle.

**Key Steps to Take in Your 60s:**

> **Start Withdrawing Your Retirement Funds Wisely:** At this stage, you may need to begin tapping into your retirement savings. Use conservative withdrawals from sources like **NPS**, **PPF**, or **SIP income**.

> **Minimize Risk:** By now, your portfolio should be predominantly in low-risk investments like **fixed income products** or **debt funds**. Avoid high-risk investments that could jeopardize your retirement funds.

> **Plan for Legacy:** If you haven't already, start planning your estate. Ensure your will is updated and your beneficiaries are clearly defined. Consider setting up a **trust** to manage your wealth and pass it on smoothly.

**Example:**

> **Sarita**, 60 years old, is withdrawing funds from her **PPF** and **NPS** to cover her monthly expenses. She has also established a **trust** for her children to ensure that her wealth is passed on according to her wishes.

**Key Takeaways:**

> **Start Early in Your 20s:** The earlier you start saving and investing, the more time your money will have to grow.

> **Maximize Contributions in Your 40s and 50s:** As you get older, focus on increasing contributions to secure your retirement future.

- ➤ **Plan for Healthcare Costs in Your 50s and 60s:** Medical expenses can rise as you age, so ensure you have comprehensive health insurance and a contingency fund.

- ➤ **Reduce Risk as You Approach Retirement:** In your 50s and 60s, shift towards safer investments like **debt funds** and **SCSS** to preserve your wealth.

- ➤ **Irregular Income:** Self-employed individuals often face inconsistent income. While this can create uncertainty, it also presents an opportunity to be strategic about savings in higher-earning months.

- ➤ **Longer Retirement Period:** As a self-employed person, you may not have access to employer-sponsored healthcare or other benefits, so planning for healthcare costs and retirement becomes even more critical.

*"The fine print in a real estate deal is where dreams turn into nightmares."* - *Anurag*

## Chapter 16:
# Real Estate Mis-selling in India

**Introduction**

Real estate has always been a preferred investment avenue for Indians, offering both security and potential appreciation. However, the sector is plagued by widespread mis selling, where developers, brokers, and financial intermediaries use deceptive tactics to lure investors into buying residential and commercial properties that may not meet their expectations. Many buyers fall prey to misleading advertisements, assured return schemes, and hidden clauses, leading to financial distress.

This chapter delves into real estate mis selling in India, covering residential and commercial property scams and the notorious 'assured return' plans. We also provide real-life examples and tips to safeguard investors from falling into such traps.

**Common Forms of Real Estate Mis selling**

**1. Misleading Advertisements**

Developers often market projects with attractive offers such as "Luxury Homes at Affordable Prices" or "Guaranteed High Returns," creating an illusion of lucrative deals. The reality, however, is often different. Amenities promised in brochures may not materialize, or project approvals may be pending, delaying possession indefinitely.

**Example:** In 2016, a prominent developer in Noida advertised luxurious apartments with top-notch amenities. However, after possession, buyers found that the promised clubhouse and swimming pool were not constructed, leading to legal disputes.

**Practical Story: Piyush**, a retired banker, invested his life savings in what was advertised as a luxury apartment complex in Pune. When he finally got possession, the society lacked basic amenities like water supply and proper roads. Struggling with legal battles and the stress of unexpected expenses, Rajesh regretted not doing thorough research before investing.

## 2. Pre-launch and Soft Launch Scams

Many developers sell properties at the "pre-launch" stage, claiming that early investors will benefit from lower prices. However, if regulatory approvals are not in place, projects may never take off, leaving investors stranded.

**Example:** The infamous Jaypee Wish Town project in Noida saw thousands of buyers investing in pre-launch offers, but due to financial troubles and legal battles, many still await their homes.

**Emotional Story: Aditya** and **Nidhi**, a newly married couple, dreamed of owning a home in a metropolitan city. They put their savings into a pre-launch project, hoping to move in before starting their family. Years passed, and the project remained incomplete. They now live in a rented house, paying both EMI and rent, emotionally and financially drained by the unpleasant experience.

## 3. Assured Return Schemes

Assured return plans promise fixed monthly returns (8-12%) on commercial or residential properties until possession. While they seem attractive, many developers fail to honour these commitments once sales targets are met, leaving investors with stalled projects and financial losses.

**Example:** In Gurugram, several commercial projects lured investors with assured return schemes but stopped payments midway, citing financial difficulties. Investors were left fighting long legal battles with little recourse.

**Practical Story: Randhir**, a middle-aged IT professional, invested in a commercial project offering assured returns, hoping to secure passive income for his children's education. The payments stopped within a year, and his legal battle has been ongoing for five years, causing immense mental distress and financial burden.

## 4. Hidden Costs and Clauses

Many buyers sign agreements without thoroughly reading the fine print, which includes hidden charges for maintenance, parking, and club memberships. Some contracts also have clauses allowing developers to delay possession without penalty.

**Example:** A builder in Bengaluru charged buyers for amenities separately despite advertising them as "inclusive" in the purchase price. Many buyers had to pay lakhs extra before getting possession.

**Emotional Story: Meera**, a single mother, saved for years to buy a 2BHK flat for her son's future. When she finally got possession, she was asked to pay unexpected fees amounting to several lakhs. The financial strain left her feeling helpless and betrayed.

## How to Protect Yourself from Real Estate Mis selling

- **Verify RERA Registration:** Before investing, check if the project is registered with the Real Estate Regulatory Authority (RERA). This ensures greater transparency and accountability.

- **Avoid Pre-launch Offers:** Do not invest in projects that do not have all regulatory approvals in place.

- **Read the Agreement Carefully:** Check for hidden costs, penalty clauses, and delivery timelines before signing.

- **Beware of Assured Returns:** If an offer seems too good to be true, it probably is. Ensure that the returns are backed by proper legal agreements.

- **Visit the Site Personally:** Do not rely solely on brochures or digital renderings; visit the project site to check actual progress.

- **Check Developer Reputation:** Research the developer's track record, past projects, and financial health before making a decision.

## Conclusion

Real estate mis selling in India has caused significant financial losses for unsuspecting investors. While regulatory reforms like RERA have improved transparency, awareness remains the key to safeguarding investments. By conducting due diligence, staying informed, and avoiding unrealistic promises, investors can make prudent real estate decisions and protect their hard-earned money from fraudulent schemes.

Through the stories of **Aditya, Nidhi, Piyush, Randhir**, and **Meera**, we see how real estate scams impact real lives. Their experiences serve as cautionary tales for prospective investors, reinforcing the importance of vigilance in real estate transactions.

*"Financial fraud is the art of making people believe in what never existed." – Anurag*

## Chapter 17:
# Awareness Regarding Financial Scams in India

**Introduction**

India has witnessed a surge in financial scams over the years, affecting individuals and businesses alike. Fraudsters use deceptive tactics, leveraging loopholes in regulations and people's lack of awareness to orchestrate scams. These fraudulent schemes have led to massive financial losses, eroding public trust in financial institutions and investment opportunities.

This chapter aims to create awareness about common financial scams in India, providing real-life examples and practical measures to safeguard against them.

**Common Financial Scams in India**

**1. Ponzi and Multi-Level Marketing (MLM) Scams**

Ponzi schemes promise high returns with little to no risk, relying on money from new investors to pay earlier investors. MLM scams operate similarly but involve selling products or services through a chain of recruits.

**Example:** The Speak Asia scam lured investors with survey-based earnings, promising lucrative returns. Eventually, it collapsed, leaving thousands of investors without their money.

**How to Avoid:**

- ➢ Verify if the investment scheme is registered with SEBI & RBI.
- ➢ Be wary of schemes guaranteeing high returns without risk.
- ➢ Avoid recruitment-based earning models.

## 2. Banking and UPI Frauds

Scammers use fake calls, phishing emails, and fraudulent UPI links to steal banking credentials and siphon money from accounts.

**Example:** Fraudsters posing as bank officials call victims, claiming their ATM card is blocked and asking for OTPs. Once the OTP is shared, money is withdrawn from the victim's account.

**How to Avoid:**

- ➢ Never share OTPs, PINs, or banking details over calls or messages.
- ➢ Verify links before clicking, especially if received via email or SMS.
- ➢ Use multi-factor authentication for banking transactions.

## 3. Stock Market and Investment Frauds

Many investors fall for stock market tips promising overnight riches, often manipulated by fraudulent advisories.

**Example:** In the Karvy Stock Broking scam, client shares were illegally pledged for loans without their knowledge, leading to significant losses.

**How to Avoid:**

- ➢ Always invest through SEBI-registered brokers.
- ➢ Avoid get-rich-quick investment tips.
- ➢ Cross-check financial advice before making decisions.

## 4. Online Loan and Instant Credit Frauds

Fraudulent loan apps promise instant credit but trap borrowers with hidden charges, high-interest rates, and harassment for repayments.

**Example:** Several Chinese-operated loan apps flooded the Indian market, exploiting borrowers and misusing their personal data for blackmail and threats.

**How to Avoid:**

- ➢ Use only RBI-approved lending platforms.
- ➢ Read the loan agreement carefully before borrowing.
- ➢ Report suspicious apps to authorities.

## 5. Cryptocurrency and Fake Investment Scams

The rise of digital currencies has led to fake crypto investment platforms and fraudulent Initial Coin Offerings (ICOs).

**Example:** The Gain Bitcoin scam, run by Amit Bhardwaj, duped investors by promising high returns on Bitcoin investments. The scam resulted in losses worth over ₹2,000 crore.

**How to Avoid:**

- ➢ Avoid schemes promising guaranteed profits in crypto trading.

➤ Verify the credentials of any crypto investment scheme.

## 6. Forex Trading Fraud in India

Foreign Exchange (Forex) trading is a global financial activity where traders exchange currencies to make profits based on fluctuations in exchange rates. While Forex trading is legal in many countries, in India, it is highly regulated by the Reserve Bank of India (RBI) and the Securities and Exchange Board of India (SEBI). Due to these restrictions, many illegal forex trading platforms have emerged, leading to fraudulent schemes that deceive investors.**Example:** Several unregulated forex trading apps such as OctaFX and Binomo were banned by RBI after they were found engaging in misleading investment practices and unauthorized transactions, leading to heavy investor losses.

➤ **Regulatory Framework in India**

Forex trading in India is governed by:

Foreign Exchange Management Act (FEMA), 1999

Reserve Bank of India (RBI) Guidelines

Securities and Exchange Board of India (SEBI) Regulations

As per FEMA, Indian residents are only allowed to trade forex through authorized dealers and exchanges like NSE, BSE, and MCX-SX that provide currency derivatives. Trading on international forex platforms or engaging with unregulated brokers is illegal.

➤ **Common Forex Trading Frauds in India**

Despite strict regulations, many individuals fall victim to fraudulent forex schemes. Some common types include:

## a) Ponzi & Multi-Level Marketing (MLM) Schemes

Fraudsters create schemes that promise high and guaranteed returns by asking investors to recruit more participants. These schemes collapse when recruitment slows, leaving investors with heavy losses.

**Example**: A company named "FXM Global" lured investors with promises of 10% monthly returns and required them to bring in more people to increase earnings. Eventually, it collapsed, and investors lost millions.

## b) Unauthorized Online Forex Trading Platforms

Many online platforms operate illegally, offering leverage-based forex trading. These platforms claim to be international brokers but often manipulate trades, leading to investor losses.

**Example:** A trader from Mumbai invested Rs. 5 lakh in an offshore forex platform promising high returns. When he tried to withdraw profits, the website disappeared, and the company ceased communication.

## c) Signal Selling Scams

Some scammers sell "premium forex signals" to traders, claiming to have insider market information. However, these signals are often random and result in losses.

**Example:** A Telegram group "Forex King Signals" charged Rs. 25,000 for trading tips, which turned out to be fake. Many traders lost money following their recommendations.

## d) Manipulated Trading Accounts

Fake brokers manipulate trading accounts by altering price feeds, increasing spreads, or preventing withdrawals.

**Example:** A forex broker "TradeMax Pro" manipulated prices to trigger stop losses and refused withdrawals. The broker was later found to be unlicensed and disappeared after defrauding hundreds of traders.

### ➢ Real-Life Cases of Forex Fraud in India

OctaFX Scam (2023): The RBI issued warnings against OctaFX, an unregistered forex platform that scammed thousands of traders.

Alpari Forex Case: A fake broker used the Alpari name to attract investors, eventually shutting down without returning funds.

### ➢ How to Identify and Avoid Forex Fraud

Red Flags of a Forex Scam

Guaranteed high returns with no risk

Unregulated or offshore broker

Pressure to invest quickly

No proper contact details or physical office

Difficulty in withdrawing funds

Preventive Measures

Trade only through authorized brokers registered with SEBI.

Verify the broker's license and regulatory approvals.

Avoid offshore forex platforms operating illegally in India.

Educate yourself on legal forex trading in India.

Report fraudulent schemes to RBI, SEBI, and law enforcement authorities.

## *Conclusion*

Forex trading fraud in India is a growing concern, with scammers exploiting regulatory loopholes and traders' lack of knowledge. The best way to protect oneself is by staying informed, following regulatory guidelines, and verifying brokers before investing. Government authorities are actively cracking down on illegal forex platforms, and traders must exercise caution to avoid financial losses.

***"If you have to hide details to make a sale, you're selling the wrong thing."*** *– Warren Buffett*

## Chapter 18:
# Insurance Mis-Selling in India

**Introduction**

Insurance is a critical financial instrument designed to provide protection against unforeseen risks. However, in India, the industry has been plagued by rampant mis-selling, which has eroded consumer trust and led to financial distress for policyholders. Mis-selling occurs when an insurance policy is sold by misrepresenting facts, providing incomplete information, or coercing individuals into buying policies that do not suit their needs.

**Understanding Insurance Mis-Selling**

Insurance mis-selling can take several forms, including:

- **Misrepresentation of Benefits**: Agents or insurers exaggerate the benefits of a policy while downplaying its limitations.

- **Selling Unsuitable Policies**: Policies are sold to customers who do not need them or cannot afford them, such as pension plans to young individuals with unstable incomes.

- **Hiding Critical Terms and Conditions**: Important policy details, such as lock-in periods, exclusions, and penalties, are often concealed.

- **Pressure Tactics**: High-pressure sales tactics are used to force customers into purchasing policies without due diligence.

- **Fake Promises and False Commitments**: Agents assure policyholders of unrealistic returns or benefits that are not part of the policy.

- **Switching Policies for Commission**: Agents persuade customers to switch policies frequently to earn higher commissions, resulting in losses due to surrender charges.

## Causes of Insurance Mis-Selling in India

Several factors contribute to the prevalence of insurance mis-selling in India:

- **Commission-Driven Sales Model**: Agents earn commissions based on sales, leading to a conflict of interest where they prioritize earnings over customer needs.

- **Lack of Consumer Awareness**: Many customers do not fully understand insurance policies, making them vulnerable to misleading sales tactics.

- **High Sales Targets**: Insurers set aggressive sales targets for agents and employees, encouraging unethical selling practices.

- **Complexity of Insurance Products**: Many policies come with intricate terms and conditions that are difficult for the average consumer to comprehend.

- **Weak Regulatory Oversight**: Despite the presence of the Insurance Regulatory and Development Authority of India (IRDAI), enforcement of strict penalties against mis-selling remains inconsistent.

## Impact of Insurance Mis-Selling

The consequences of insurance mis-selling can be severe and far-reaching:

- **Financial Losses for Consumers**: Policyholders end up paying premiums for policies that do not serve their intended purpose.

- **Loss of Trust in the Insurance Sector**: Widespread mis-selling reduces confidence in the insurance industry.

- **Regulatory Burden**: The IRDAI must allocate additional resources to monitor and address mis-selling complaints.

- **Legal Disputes**: Many mis-sold policies result in legal battles, adding to the burden on the judiciary.

- **Reduction in Insurance Penetration**: Negative experiences discourage people from purchasing insurance, affecting financial security at a national level.

## Regulatory Measures to Curb Mis-Selling

Recognizing the issue, the IRDAI and the government have introduced several measures to control mis-selling:

- **Tighter Regulations**: IRDAI has mandated stricter disclosure norms, ensuring consumers receive complete information.

- **Cooling-Off Period (Free Look Period)**: Policyholders can cancel a policy within 15-30 days if they feel it was mis-sold.

- ➤ **Mandatory Training for Agents**: Insurance agents are required to undergo training and pass examinations before being certified.

- ➤ **Grievance Redressal Mechanisms**: Platforms like the Insurance Ombudsman and IRDAI grievance cells offer policyholders avenues for complaint resolution.

- ➤ **Standardization of Products**: IRDAI has introduced simplified insurance products with clear terms to help consumers make informed decisions.

## Steps Consumers Can Take to Avoid Mis-Selling

Consumers must also take proactive steps to safeguard themselves from falling prey to mis-selling:

- ➤ **Educate Themselves About Insurance Products**: Understanding different policies and their terms can prevent misinformation.

- ➤ **Read Policy Documents Carefully**: Checking for hidden charges, exclusions, and lock-in periods is crucial.

- ➤ **Avoid Rushed Decisions**: Taking time to compare policies before purchasing helps in making informed choices.

- ➤ **Verify the Credibility of Agents**: Ensuring that the agent is IRDAI-certified and checking their track record can minimize risks.

- ➤ **Utilize Online Comparison Platforms**: Digital platforms provide unbiased comparisons of policies.

- ➤ **Exercise Free Look Period Rights**: If a policy seems misrepresented, consumers should utilize the free look period for cancellations.

➢ **Expert Advice**: Consult experience financial consultant before buying such policies.

## Conclusion

Insurance mis-selling in India remains a serious challenge, affecting consumers, insurers, and the overall financial ecosystem. While regulatory bodies have taken significant steps to curb malpractices, a collaborative effort involving policymakers, insurers, and consumers is essential to ensure ethical sales practices. Awareness, transparency, and strict enforcement of laws will be key to mitigating the issue and restoring trust in the insurance industry.

*"A financial advisor helps you avoid expensive lessons the market is waiting to teach you."-Anurag*

## Chapter 19:
# The Role of a Financial Advisor in Retirement Planning

**Introduction**

Retirement planning is a complex process that requires careful decision-making. A financial advisor plays a crucial role in helping individuals navigate investment choices, tax implications, and withdrawal strategies to ensure a stable and secure retirement.

**Why a Financial Advisor is Important**

- ➢ They help structure retirement savings for longevity.
- ➢ Provide expert guidance on asset allocation and tax efficiency.
- ➢ Assist in adapting to economic changes and inflation.
- ➢ Reduce emotional decision-making by offering objective financial advice.

## Benefits of Hiring a Financial Advisor

### 1. Personalized Retirement Strategy
- Tailored investment and withdrawal plans based on individual goals.
- Strategies that balance growth and security.

### 2. Tax Optimization
- Guidance on tax-efficient withdrawal strategies.
- Minimizing tax liability on pensions, annuities, and investments.

### 3. Risk Management
- Diversified investment portfolio for risk reduction.
- Adjusting asset allocation as retirement progresses.

### 4. Long-Term Care and Estate Planning
- Planning for medical expenses and long-term care.
- Assistance with wills, trusts, and inheritance planning.

### 5. Adjusting to Market Conditions
- Managing investments in response to market fluctuations.
- Ensuring sustainable income flow even during downturns.

## How to Choose the Right Financial Advisor
- Look for SEBI-registered financial advisors.
- Evaluate their experience and track record.
- Understand their fee structure (commission-based vs. fee-only).

- ➤ Ensure transparency and alignment with personal financial goals.
- ➤ Seek referrals and read client reviews for credibility.

**Common Mistakes to Avoid When Hiring an Advisor**

- ➤ Choosing an advisor based on low fees rather than expertise.
- ➤ Not verifying credentials or experience.
- ➤ Ignoring conflicts of interest in commission-based advisors.
- ➤ Failing to review the advisor's investment philosophy.

**Conclusion**

A financial advisor provides invaluable guidance in making well-informed decisions for retirement. From investment planning to risk management, having a trusted professional can help retirees enjoy financial security and peace of mind. Choosing the right advisor is critical, as they can provide financial stability, confidence, and a stress-free retirement experience.

*"The best time to plant a tree was 20 years ago. The second-best time is now."* – *Anurag*

## Chapter 20:
# Challenges in Retirement Planning

Retirement planning in India faces several unique challenges, primarily due to socio-economic, cultural, and financial factors. As life expectancy increases and families become more dispersed, individuals need to be proactive in ensuring that they can live comfortably after retirement. Here are some key challenges in retirement planning that need to be addressed for a secure and prosperous future:

### 1. Lack of Awareness and Financial Literacy

One of the biggest hurdles in India is the general lack of awareness about the need for retirement planning. Many people are unaware of how much they should save, where to invest, and what options are available. There is also a general lack of financial literacy, which makes it difficult for individuals to understand financial products like NPS (National Pension System), EPF (Employees' Provident Fund), PPF (Public Provident Fund), and other long-term investment instruments.

**Solution**: Financial education campaigns, workshops, and more accessible resources for financial literacy can help bridge this gap. It's essential to teach people how to assess their retirement needs, create a savings plan, and invest accordingly.

## 2. Unpredictable Inflation

India has experienced rising inflation rates, particularly in essential sectors like healthcare, housing, and education. This makes it challenging to estimate the amount needed for retirement. With inflation, the value of money decreases over time, reducing the purchasing power of an individual's savings.

**Solution**: To counter this, individuals should invest in inflation-beating assets such as equities, gold, or mutual funds. It's important to regularly review retirement goals to adjust for inflationary trends and ensure that retirement corpus grows accordingly.

## 3. Inadequate Government Support

Unlike some western countries where pension schemes are robust and provide substantial support post-retirement, India's pension system is relatively underdeveloped. The government's contribution through EPF and NPS is limited, and not everyone participates in these systems, particularly in the unorganized sector.

**Solution**: A more inclusive and comprehensive pension system is needed, along with incentivizing the unorganized sector to participate in pension schemes. Individuals should also consider supplementary private retirement savings options like mutual funds, NPS, and other long-term financial products.

## 4. Dependency on Family Support

Traditionally, the elderly in India have relied on family support during their retirement years. However, the changing family structure—with smaller families, nuclear setups, and children living in different cities or abroad—means that many seniors may not have the same level of support from their children.

**Solution**: It's important to emphasize self-sufficiency and encourage individuals to save for retirement from an early age. Additionally, creating a retirement plan that does not depend solely on family support is crucial. This can include annuities or other guaranteed income streams.

## 5. Limited Investment Options

While the Indian investment landscape has evolved with more sophisticated options such as stocks, bonds, mutual funds, and real estate, there still exists a general preference for low-risk options like fixed deposits or gold. Many people are risk-averse and prefer to keep their savings in traditional instruments, which may not generate the kind of returns required to sustain a comfortable retirement.

**Solution**: A balanced approach to risk is essential. Encouraging people to diversify their portfolios and gradually move towards higher-return assets like equities, mutual funds, or NPS will help them build a more substantial retirement corpus.

## 6. Healthcare Costs

In India, medical expenses can be a significant burden in retirement. With age, the likelihood of health problems increases, and healthcare costs rise sharply. The absence of universal healthcare coverage and high out-of-pocket expenses further exacerbates this problem.

**Solution**: It is crucial for individuals to factor healthcare costs into their retirement planning. Comprehensive health insurance and emergency savings should be part of the retirement corpus. A combination of a long-term health plan and personal savings can reduce the financial burden in later years.

## 7. Economic Uncertainty

Fluctuating economic conditions, market volatility, and global events (like the COVID-19 pandemic) can affect savings and investments. Uncertainty in the economy makes it difficult to predict long-term financial outcomes, which can lead to insecurity regarding retirement.

**Solution**: A diversified investment strategy, regular portfolio reviews, and risk management are key to mitigating economic uncertainties. People should focus on building a robust emergency fund to deal with financial disruptions.

## 8. Late Start in Saving and Investing

Many people in India tend to delay saving for retirement. They prioritize short-term needs or spend heavily in their younger years, leaving little room for long-term planning. The younger workforce often feels that retirement is too far away to start saving seriously, leading to missed opportunities for wealth compounding.

**Solution**: Starting early is the key to retirement planning. Even small, consistent contributions to retirement savings can grow over time due to the power of compounding. Employers can also play a vital role in encouraging employees to begin saving by offering employer-sponsored retirement schemes or incentives to participate in NPS or EPF.

## 9. Changing Retirement Age

In India, the retirement age is typically 58 to 60 years for government employees, but the private sector does not have a standard retirement age. As a result, many individuals may not have a fixed end to their working life, which complicates the retirement planning process. Moreover, increasing life expectancy means that people may need to plan for a retirement period that lasts 20-30 years or longer.

**Solution**: Individuals should focus on flexibility in their retirement plans. This could include considering early retirement, starting a second career, or part-time work to supplement retirement income. Planning for a longer lifespan means building a retirement fund that can withstand a longer post-retirement phase.

## Conclusion

Retirement planning in India comes with its own set of challenges, but with the right strategies, these obstacles can be overcome. Awareness, education, and financial discipline are key components of a successful retirement plan. It's crucial to start early, diversify investments, and ensure that healthcare and inflation are adequately accounted for. By recognizing these challenges and proactively addressing them, individuals can secure a comfortable and financially stable retirement.

*"The best way to show love for your family is to ensure they don't have to fight over your estate." -Anurag*

## Chapter 21:
# The Importance of Estate Planning & Legacy Building in Retirement Planning

Retirement planning is often associated with securing financial independence for one's later years, ensuring that the golden years are filled with peace, comfort, and stability. However, one crucial aspect that often gets overlooked in retirement planning is **Estate planning** and **legacy building**. These two elements are vital in ensuring that your assets are passed on to the next generation in the most efficient and meaningful way possible.

## What is Estate Planning?

Estate planning is the process of organizing and arranging for the distribution of your assets after you pass away. It involves legal and financial strategies to ensure that your wishes are followed regarding who receives your property, how your debts are settled, and how your estate will be managed.

Estate planning typically includes several key documents:

> - **Will**: A legal document that outlines how your assets will be distributed after your death. It also designates guardians for your minor children, if any.

- **Trust**: A legal arrangement that allows you to transfer assets to a trustee for the benefit of your beneficiaries. Trusts can help avoid probate, minimize taxes, and ensure assets are distributed according to your wishes.

- **Power of Attorney**: A document that designates someone to make financial and medical decisions on your behalf if you're unable to do so due to illness or incapacity.

- **Living Will/Advance Healthcare Directive**: A document that outlines your preferences for medical treatment should you become incapacitated.

By establishing an estate plan, you ensure that your assets are distributed according to your wishes, reduce the burden on your family during a difficult time, and potentially minimize taxes and legal fees associated with transferring your estate.

## Why is Estate Planning Crucial in Retirement?

- **Protecting Your Assets**: As you approach retirement, your accumulated assets—whether in real estate, savings, investments, or business become valuable resources. Estate planning ensures these assets are protected and passed on without unnecessary delays or complications.

- **Avoiding Family Disputes**: Without clear instructions in the form of a will or trust, your loved ones may face disputes over your estate. A well-structured estate plan provides clarity and prevents potential conflicts within your family.

- **Minimizing Tax Liabilities**: In India, inheritance tax does not exist, but your estate may still be subject to other taxes such as capital gains tax or estate duty (for certain estates). Proper planning can help reduce the tax burden on your heirs and ensure that your wealth is transferred as efficiently as possible.

- **Providing for Loved Ones**: Estate planning ensures that your family members, dependents, and loved ones are financially cared for, especially if you're no longer around to provide for them. This is particularly important for children, elderly parents, or anyone relying on you for financial support.

## Legacy Building: Leaving a Mark

Legacy building goes beyond just passing on material wealth—it's about creating an enduring impact that reflects your values, beliefs, and achievements. It involves instilling principles that will continue to benefit future generations and shaping the legacy you leave behind.

Building a legacy is about:

- **Financial Legacy**: The most common aspect of legacy building is ensuring that your wealth is passed down in a way that helps future generations. This can involve creating educational trusts for children or grandchildren, funding charitable causes, or setting up endowments.

- **Philanthropy**: Many individuals choose to create a philanthropic legacy by supporting charitable organizations, causes, or projects that align with their values. Charitable giving, whether through direct donations or through the creation of a foundation or trust, can have a profound impact on society and reflect your desire to contribute to the greater good.

> **Cultural and Family Legacy**: A legacy isn't only about financial wealth. It's also about passing on the values, traditions, and lessons learned throughout your life. Creating a family history, writing memoirs, or establishing family traditions can help future generations stay connected with their roots and the guiding principles that shaped their lives.

> **Values and Ethics**: The legacy you leave behind can shape the character of future generations. Teaching your children and grandchildren the importance of hard work, integrity, financial responsibility, and kindness is a form of legacy that goes beyond material wealth.

> **Mentorship and Knowledge Transfer**: Sharing your wisdom, skills, and experience with others is another powerful way of building a legacy. As you move toward retirement, consider passing down your knowledge to younger family members or mentoring others in your community. This creates a lasting impact that can last long after you've retired.

## Key Steps in Estate Planning and Legacy Building

> **Assess Your Assets and Liabilities**: Begin by reviewing all of your assets, such as property, investments, savings, and business holdings. Also, consider any debts you may have. This assessment will help you understand the scope of your estate and plan accordingly.

> **Create a Will and Trust**: Decide how you want your assets to be distributed, and create a legally binding will or trust to ensure that your wishes are respected. A trust can also help you avoid lengthy probate processes.

> **Designate Beneficiaries**: Ensure that all your accounts (bank accounts, retirement funds,

insurance policies) have designated beneficiaries to ensure they are passed on directly without delays.

- **Plan for Healthcare Decisions**: Establish a healthcare directive and a power of attorney to ensure your medical wishes are respected should you be unable to communicate them yourself.
- **Consider Charitable Giving**: If leaving a philanthropic legacy is important to you, look into various giving strategies, such as setting up charitable trusts, making regular donations, or creating endowments for causes close to your heart.
- **Communicate with Family**: Make sure that your family is aware of your estate planning decisions. Clear communication can help ensure there are no misunderstandings and that your wishes are followed.
- **Review and Update**: Estate planning isn't a one-time task—it should be reviewed periodically, especially after major life events like the birth of children, changes in financial circumstances, or retirement.

## Conclusion

Estate planning and legacy building are critical components of a comprehensive retirement plan. They ensure that your wealth and values are passed down in a manner that reflects your desires and provides security for your loved ones. By carefully planning your estate, you can avoid unnecessary complications, reduce tax liabilities, and leave a meaningful legacy that can positively impact future generations. In doing so, you will not only protect your wealth but also make a lasting impact on the world.

## *The Price of Unplanned Retirement: A Lesson from Vijaypat Singhania's Journey*

***Vijaypat Singhania***, once the celebrated chairman of Raymond Group, was a man of vision and determination. Under his leadership, Raymond became a household name in the textile industry, synonymous with luxury and elegance. But despite his remarkable success, his later years were marred by financial and personal struggles, largely due to inadequate retirement planning.

At the peak of his career, Singhania was among India's wealthiest industrialists. His business acumen and strategic decisions had turned Raymond into a billion-dollar empire. However, his biggest miscalculation was assuming that familial bonds would be enough to secure his post-retirement life.

Believing in the power of family, he decided to transfer the control of his company to his son, ***Gautam Singhania***, in 2015. It was a move that many saw as an act of faith, but it soon turned into a cautionary tale. Without a proper financial safety net or a well-structured retirement plan, ***Vijaypat*** found himself in a vulnerable position. The father-son relationship deteriorated, leading to legal disputes and public controversies. The man who once owned a business empire was now struggling for financial stability.

This story serves as a crucial lesson for professionals and business owners: wealth today does not guarantee security tomorrow. Effective retirement planning is not just about accumulating wealth but ensuring that assets are structured to provide lifelong financial independence.

Here are some key takeaways from ***Vijaypat Singhania's*** experience:

- **Retain Financial Independence** – No matter how much wealth you amass, always keep a portion of your asset's liquid and under your control. Diversify investments across fixed-income instruments, real estate, and mutual funds to create a steady income stream.

- **Legal Safeguards Are Essential** – Retirement planning should involve strong legal frameworks, including wills, trusts, and succession planning. A lack of clarity in legal matters can lead to disputes that can erode both wealth and relationships.

- **Plan Beyond Family Dynamics** – While it is natural to trust family members, financial decisions should be made objectively. Relying solely on family without formalized financial structures can be risky.

- **Lifestyle Adjustments** – As one transitions into retirement, financial planning should include budgeting for healthcare, travel, and daily expenses, ensuring that one's lifestyle is maintained without dependency.

- **Seek Professional Guidance** – Retirement planning is complex and should not be left to assumptions. Consulting financial advisors, wealth managers, and legal experts can prevent costly mistakes.

*Vijaypat Singhania's* story is a stark reminder that retirement planning is not just for the salaried middle class but also for the ultra-wealthy. No matter how successful one may be, a well-planned retirement strategy is crucial to ensuring dignity and financial stability in the later years of life.

*"The best time to act was yesterday. The second-best time is right now."* -Anurag

## Chapter 22: Conclusion and Action Plan for Retirement Planning

Retirement planning is an essential but often overlooked aspect of financial management. As we face rising life expectancy, changing family dynamics, and an unpredictable economic environment, the need for a well-thought-out retirement plan has never been more critical. Whether you are just beginning your career, in the midst of it, or nearing retirement, it's never too late to start planning for your future. The good news is that with proper knowledge, discipline, and consistent effort, anyone can build a secure and comfortable retirement.

**Key Takeaways**

> - **Early Planning is Crucial**: The sooner you start, the better. Starting early allows you to take advantage of the power of compounding, giving your investments time to grow. Even small contributions can lead to substantial growth over time.
>
> - **The Importance of Diversification**: Diversifying your retirement savings across different asset classes—such as equities, fixed-income instruments, and real estate—helps mitigate risks and maximizes returns over the long term.

> **Inflation and Healthcare Costs**: Inflation and rising healthcare costs are critical factors that must be accounted for in your retirement planning. Ensuring that your retirement fund grows at a rate that outpaces inflation is necessary to maintain purchasing power.

> **Government Schemes and Private Investments**: Utilize government-backed schemes such as EPF, PPF, and NPS, but don't rely solely on them. Consider supplementing these with private investments in mutual funds, stocks, or real estate.

> **Self-Sufficiency is Key**: In today's changing family structures, relying solely on family support during retirement may not be a viable option. It's essential to be financially self-sufficient, ensuring you can meet your needs without burdening loved ones.

> **Regular Reviews and Adjustments**: Your retirement plan should not be static. Regularly reviewing your progress, adjusting your investments based on your risk appetite, and updating your goals as life circumstances change are vital steps.

## Action Plan for Retirement Planning

Creating and executing an action plan for retirement requires careful consideration of your goals, current financial situation, and future needs. Here is a step-by-step action plan to guide you:

## Step 1: Assess Your Retirement Goals

Begin by identifying your retirement goals:

> **When do you want to retire?** Decide the age at which you wish to retire. Keep in mind that retiring

earlier than the standard retirement age may require more savings.

- **What lifestyle do you envision?** Consider your desired lifestyle, including housing, travel, hobbies, and leisure activities. Estimate the monthly expenses during retirement.

- **How long do you expect to live post-retirement?** With life expectancy rising, plan for a retirement phase that could last 20, 30, or even 40 years.

## Step 2: Calculate the Amount You Need

Next, calculate the amount of money you need to accumulate for retirement. Consider the following:

- **Estimate your retirement expenses**: Consider daily living expenses, healthcare, travel, and any other liabilities. Adjust for inflation to ensure your funds will maintain purchasing power.

- **Factor in healthcare costs**: Make provisions for rising medical costs, which are often a significant part of retirement expenses.

- **Assess your income sources**: Consider income streams from pensions, EPF, NPS, social security (if applicable), or family. Determine any gaps between the required retirement amount and the funds available from these sources.

## Step 3: Start Saving and Invest Early

It's crucial to start saving for retirement as early as possible. Consider:

- **EPF (Employees' Provident Fund)**: Ensure you're contributing to EPF if you're employed in the organized sector. The contributions are tax-free, and the corpus grows over time with compounded interest.

> **PPF (Public Provident Fund)**: A low-risk, long-term savings option with tax benefits. PPF allows you to save systematically while earning attractive interest rates.

> **NPS (National Pension System)**: This government-backed pension scheme allows for voluntary contributions, providing a robust retirement solution with tax advantages.

> **Mutual Funds**: Consider investing in equity and debt mutual funds to diversify your retirement portfolio. SIPs (Systematic Investment Plans) are an effective way to build a retirement fund over time.

> **Real Estate**: If feasible, investing in property can help build wealth. Consider real estate as part of your long-term retirement planning, but ensure that it aligns with your risk appetite.

## Step 4: Build an Emergency Fund

Set aside 6 to 12 months' worth of living expenses in a liquid, easily accessible fund to cover any unexpected expenses, such as medical emergencies or short-term financial setbacks. This will ensure that your retirement savings remain intact and are not compromised.

## Step 5: Manage Debt and Expenses

Debt can derail your retirement plan. Prioritize paying off high-interest debts, such as credit card debt, personal loans, or consumer loans. Keeping your expenses under control and reducing unnecessary expenditures will allow you to save more for retirement.

## Step 6: Review Your Investments Regularly

As you progress through your career, your financial goals, risk tolerance, and income will likely evolve. Periodically review your investments and make adjustments as needed:

- **Rebalance your portfolio** to align with your changing risk profile.
- **Increase your contribution** as your income grows or as you near retirement.
- **Monitor inflation** and adjust your savings goals to ensure your retirement corpus keeps pace with the cost of living.

## Step 7: Prepare for Healthcare Needs

Healthcare costs tend to rise significantly with age. Consider these strategies:

- **Health Insurance**: Invest in a comprehensive health insurance policy to cover medical emergencies.
- **Critical Illness Insurance**: This can help cover the costs of serious diseases like cancer, heart disease, or kidney failure.
- **Long-Term Care Plans**: These plans are designed to cover expenses for individuals who need assistance with daily living activities due to age or illness.

## Step 8: Plan for the Unexpected

While we can't predict the future, it's essential to plan for unexpected events, such as the death of a spouse or a health crisis. Consider life insurance and critical illness cover to protect your family and ensure that your retirement savings are not depleted by unforeseen circumstances.

## Step 9: Educate Your Family

Retirement planning should not just be an individual endeavour. Educate your family, especially your spouse and children, about your retirement goals and the importance of saving. This will help avoid misunderstandings in the future and ensure that everyone is aligned with your financial plans.

## Step 10: Seek Professional Advice

As your portfolio grows and becomes more complex, consulting with a financial planner or retirement advisor can help ensure that you're on track to meet your goals. A professional can offer personalized advice, help you with tax optimization, and suggest strategies to maximize your retirement savings.

## Conclusion

Retirement planning is a continuous and evolving process that requires careful consideration of various factors, from lifestyle goals to investment strategies. By starting early, staying disciplined, and regularly reviewing your plan, you can ensure that you will enjoy a financially secure and comfortable retirement. The key to successful retirement planning lies in taking proactive steps today to secure a stable and fulfilling future.

Remember, it's not just about saving money—it's about making informed decisions, diversifying your investments, and taking control of your financial future. Take the first step now, and your future self will thank you.

## Key Notes: Retirement Withdrawals and Distribution Strategies

## Introduction

Retirement planning is not just about saving money—it's also about how to withdraw and distribute your savings efficiently. A well-structured withdrawal strategy ensures that your money lasts throughout your retirement while minimizing tax liabilities and maximizing returns.

**Key Withdrawal Strategies**

**1. Systematic Withdrawal Plan (SWP)**

- Ideal for retirees relying on mutual funds.
- Provides regular cash flow while keeping the principal invested.
- Helps manage market volatility and tax implications.

**2. The 6% Rule**

- A widely accepted rule stating that withdrawing 6% of your retirement corpus annually allows it to last 25-30 years.
- Adjustments may be needed for inflation and market fluctuations.

**3. Bucket Strategy**

- Segments your retirement savings into three buckets:
  - **Short-term (0-5 years):** Low-risk investments like fixed deposits (FDs) and savings accounts.
  - **Mid-term (5-10 years):** Moderate-risk investments such as Hybrid Mutual funds.
  - **Long-term (10+ years):** Higher-risk investments like aggressive Mutual funds and Real Estate.

## 4. Required Minimum Distributions (RMDs) for NPS and EPF

➢ National Pension System (NPS) mandates 40% corpus allocation to annuities upon retirement.

➢ Employees' Provident Fund (EPF) withdrawals are tax-free under specific conditions.

➢ Planning withdrawals to minimize tax burden is crucial.

**Tax-Efficient Withdrawal Strategies**

➢ Withdraw from tax-free investments (PPF, EPF) first.

➢ Plan NPS withdrawals carefully to balance lump sum and annuity payouts.

➢ Optimize withdrawals to stay within lower tax brackets.

**Conclusion**

Choosing the right withdrawal strategy can make a significant difference in the sustainability of your retirement savings. A combination of strategies based on risk appetite and financial needs can ensure a comfortable retirement.

**Key Notes: Health and Long-Term Care Planning**

**Introduction**

Health expenses are one of the most significant financial burdens in retirement. Without proper planning, medical costs can rapidly deplete savings. Understanding health insurance, medical expenses, and long-term care planning is essential.

## Health Insurance for Retirees

### 1. Senior Citizen Health Insurance

- Special plans designed for individuals over 60.
- Covers hospitalization, critical illnesses, and pre-existing conditions with waiting periods.

### 2. Employer-Provided Coverage & Continuation Options

- Some companies offer post-retirement health benefits.
- Options like group health plans should be evaluated.

### 3. Government Schemes

- **Ayushman Bharat (PM-JAY):** Free healthcare for eligible retirees.
- **CGHS & ECHS:** Health schemes for government and defence retirees.

## Long-Term Care Considerations

### 1. Nursing Home and Home Care Expenses

- Costs for assisted living or nursing homes can be high.
- Evaluating options like reverse mortgages for funding can be beneficial.

### 2. Critical Illness and Long-Term Care Insurance

- Policies covering diseases like cancer, stroke, and Alzheimer's.
- Helps reduce out-of-pocket expenses for chronic conditions.

### 3. Emergency Medical Fund

- ➢ Keeping a separate emergency corpus for unexpected health expenses.
- ➢ Ensuring liquidity for quick access.

### Conclusion

Healthcare costs in retirement can be overwhelming. Planning ahead with insurance, savings, and government schemes can ease financial pressure and ensure a secure future.

### Key Notes: The Psychology of Retirement

### Introduction

Retirement is not just a financial shift; it's a major life transition. Many retirees face emotional challenges such as loss of identity, boredom, and lack of purpose. Understanding the psychological aspects of retirement is key to a happy and fulfilling post-work life.

### Emotional and Psychological Challenges

### 1. Loss of Identity

- ➢ Many individuals define themselves by their careers.
- ➢ Retirement can lead to feelings of loss and lack of purpose.

### 2. Social Isolation

- ➢ Work provides social interactions; post-retirement, this decreases.
- ➢ Building a social network outside work is crucial.

### 3. Fear of Running Out of Money

> ➢ Financial anxiety can affect mental well-being.

> ➢ Proper planning can reduce stress and enhance confidence.

## Strategies for a Happy Retirement

### 1. Developing New Hobbies and Interests

> ➢ Engaging in activities like travel, gardening, or learning new skills.

> ➢ Volunteering and community involvement can provide a sense of fulfilment.

### 2. Maintaining Physical and Mental Health

> ➢ Regular exercise and healthy eating promote longevity.

> ➢ Meditation and mindfulness help in mental well-being.

### 3. Strengthening Relationships

> ➢ Spending quality time with family and friends.

> ➢ Building new social circles through clubs, travel, and social gatherings.

## Conclusion

Retirement is a new phase of life that requires mental and emotional preparation. By embracing new opportunities and maintaining a balanced lifestyle, retirees can enjoy a fulfilling and joyful retirement.

## *Retire Riches Club*

Anurag Mishra, a seasoned investment expert and founder of ***Retire Riches Club***, hails from Ajmer, Rajasthan—a land of royal heritage, entrepreneurial spirit, and timeless financial wisdom. Growing up amidst the grandeur of Rajasthan's traditions, he was deeply influenced by the region's & values of discipline, prudence, and wealth preservation. The Rajasthani communities have long been known for their sharp financial acumen, and Anurag carries forward this legacy by helping individuals build sustainable wealth with smart investment strategies.

With over 15 years of hands-on experience in investments, he has developed a profound understanding of wealth management, financial planning, and the importance of long-term financial security. His expertise has empowered countless individuals to achieve financial independence, ensuring they can retire with dignity and prosperity.

Through ***Retire Riches Club***, Anurag continues to uphold the Rajasthani ethos of financial foresight and security, guiding individuals toward a future where wealth is not just built, but preserved and passed on for generations.

***Retire Riches Club*** is not just a platform; it's a dream nurtured for those who dare to believe in a secure and prosperous future. Here, we don't just invest—we build legacies, we protect dreams, and we empower you to live life on your own terms. It's a community where the wisdom of experience and the power of informed decisions come together to create a brighter tomorrow. At ***Retire Riches Club***, your journey to financial freedom becomes a shared purpose, a promise that you will retire not just with wealth, but with peace of mind and the joy of a life well-lived.

## *Retire Riches Club*: **Your Gateway to Financial Freedom**

Are you dreaming of a life where financial independence allows you to live on your own terms? The *Retire Riches Club* is here to make that dream a reality. We are a community of like-minded individuals who are committed to building wealth, achieving financial freedom, and living a life of abundance.

### About *Retire Riches Club*

The *Retire Riches Club* is more than just a membership—it's a movement. Founded on the principles of smart investing, financial education, and wealth-building strategies, our mission is to empower individuals to create long-term financial security and enjoy a rich, fulfilling retirement. Whether you're just starting your wealth journey or are a seasoned investor, this club provides tools, resources, and a network to help you maximize your potential.

## Joining Benefits

By joining the ***Retire Riches Club***, you gain access to an exclusive suite of benefits designed to help you grow and manage your wealth effectively.

### 1. Exclusive Financial Education

- ➤ Access to in-depth courses, webinars, and workshops led by industry experts.
- ➤ Step-by-step guides on budgeting, investing, and building passive income streams.
- ➤ Strategies tailored to individuals at different financial stages.

### 2. Investment Opportunities

- ➤ Early access to vetted, high-potential investment opportunities, including stocks, real estate, mutual funds, and startups.
- ➤ Expert analysis and personalized advice on managing your investment portfolio.

### 3. Personalized Wealth Planning

- ➤ Customized retirement plans and financial strategies based on your goals and lifestyle aspirations.
- ➤ Direct consultations with certified financial advisors to help optimize your finances.

### 4. Community and Networking

- ➤ Join a vibrant network of ambitious professionals and successful entrepreneurs.
- ➤ Participate in mastermind groups, forums, and exclusive events for knowledge sharing and collaboration.

## 5. Access to Wealth-Building Tools

- ➢ Cutting-edge tools to track your financial growth, assess investments, and project future wealth.

- ➢ Regular updates on market trends, economic changes, and actionable tips to grow your portfolio.

## 6. Passive Income Strategies

- ➢ Learn how to generate and scale multiple streams of passive income.

- ➢ Guidance on diversifying your income sources to create long-term stability.

## *Who Can Join the Retire Riches Club?*

- ❖ Salaried Professionals who want to build long-term wealth.
- ❖ Business Owners looking for effective financial strategies.
- ❖ Young Professionals eager to start investing early.
- ❖ Retirees who want to manage and grow their wealth post-retirement.
- ❖ Homemakers looking to contribute to family wealth creation.
- ❖ Freelancers and Gig Workers seeking financial stability.
- ❖ Doctors and Medical Professionals looking for investment guidance.
- ❖ Engineers and IT Professionals interested in wealth-building strategies.
- ❖ Authors, Teachers and Educators planning a secure financial future.
- ❖ Lawyers and Legal Professionals seeking financial security.
- ❖ Entrepreneurs looking to scale and secure their financial future.
- ❖ Astrologers, Vastu Experts, and Healers seeking financial growth.
- ❖ Travelers looking for financial freedom to support their lifestyle.
- ❖ Retired Government Officials from Army, Air Force, Navy, and NSG seeking financial security.

❖ Anyone who dreams of a financially free and stress-free future!

## *Why Choose Retire Riches Club?*

The **Retire Riches Club** is committed to making financial freedom accessible and achievable for everyone. With a proven track record of success stories, a supportive community, and an abundance of resources, joining this club is your first step towards a life of financial independence.

## How to Join

Membership in the **Retire Riches Club** is simple and rewarding. Visit our website, select the membership plan that aligns with your goals, and gain instant access to all the resources you need to retire rich.

**Take Charge of Your Financial Future Today** Don't wait for the perfect moment—create it. Join the Retire Rich Club and start building the life you deserve. Your journey to financial freedom begins now!

The **"Retire Riches Club"** typically offers different membership options to cater to various levels of interest, expertise, and goals related to financial planning and investment. While the exact types of membership might differ, here are some common ones that could be available for such a club:

1. **Basic Membership:**
   - Ideal for beginners who are just starting their financial journey.
   - Access to introductory resources and tools.
   - Basic investment tips and financial education.
   - Limited access to webinars and live sessions.

2. **Premium Membership:**
   - Suitable for those with some experience in investments.
   - Includes access to advanced investment strategies, reports, and financial tools.
   - Priority access to webinars, masterclasses, and expert-led sessions.
   - One-on-one coaching or consultations.

3. **Elite Membership:**
   - Designed for experienced investors and those looking to take their wealth-building strategy to the next level.
   - Personalized financial planning and strategies.
   - VIP access to exclusive content, events, and networking opportunities.
   - Direct access to expert mentors and advisors for detailed guidance.

4. **Corporate Membership:**
   - Targeted at businesses and organizations looking to offer financial education and planning resources to employees.
   - Group discounts and access to corporate-focused webinars and events.
   - Tailored financial wellness programs for staff members.

## 5. Lifetime Membership:

- A one-time payment for lifetime access to all club resources and events.
- Includes all the benefits of premium and elite memberships, with lifetime support and updates.

## Frequently Asked Questions (FAQs) – *Retire Riches Club*

### 1. What is Retire Riches Club?

*Retire Riches Club* is a platform designed to help individuals plan and manage their finances with the goal of achieving financial independence and retiring comfortably. It offers expert guidance, investment strategies, and tools to ensure long-term financial growth and security.

### 2. Who is the founder of Retires Riches Club?

*Retire Riches Club* was founded by Anurag Mishra, a seasoned financial expert with over 15+ years of experience in investment strategies and retirement planning.

### 3. How can Retire Riches Club help me plan for retirement?

*Retire Riches Club* provides a range of services, including personalized investment plans, financial education, portfolio management, and strategies to grow your wealth. The goal is to help you retire with peace of mind, knowing that your financial future is secure.

### 4. Do I need to be an expert to use Retire Riches Club?

No, you don't need to be a financial expert. *Retire Riches Club* is designed for people at all stages of their financial journey, from beginners to seasoned investors. The platform offers user-friendly resources, workshops, and expert support to guide you in making informed decisions.

### 5. What kind of investment strategies does Retire Riches Club offer?

*Retire Riches Club* focuses on diversified investment strategies tailored to your risk profile, goals, and time horizon. These strategies may include stocks, bonds, real estate, mutual funds, and other wealth-building vehicles to help you maximize your returns over time.

## 6. Can I get personalized investment advice from Retire Riches Club?

Yes, ***Retire Riches Club*** offers personalized financial planning and investment advice. Whether you are planning for early retirement, seeking tax-efficient growth, or aiming for other financial goals, Anurag Mishra and the team provide customized strategies for your needs.

## 7. Is there a membership fee for Retire Riches Club?

***Retire Riches Club*** offers various membership tiers with different benefits. Some services may be available for free, while premium members can access exclusive resources, one-on-one consultations, and specialized investment plans.

## 8. How do I join Retire Riches Club?

You can join ***Retire Riches Club*** by signing up on our website. After registering, you'll gain access to our resources, tools, and ongoing support for planning your financial future.

## 9. What educational resources are available on Retire Riches Club?

***Retire Riches Club*** offers webinars, workshops, articles, guides, and financial planning tools designed to educate members about effective retirement planning, investment options, and wealth management strategies.

## 10. Can Retire Riches Club help me with tax planning?

Yes, ***Retire Riches Club*** offers guidance on tax-efficient investing and retirement planning. The team helps you understand strategies to minimize taxes on your investments, maximize deductions, and optimize your overall financial situation.

## 11. Is Retire Riches Club only for people planning for retirement?

While the focus is on retirement planning, ***Retire Riches Club*** also helps individuals looking to improve their overall financial situation, such as growing wealth, managing debt, or building an emergency fund. It's about achieving financial security at any stage of life.

## 12. How can I get in touch with an expert from Retire Riches Club?

You can contact an expert from ***Retire Riches Club*** through the website's contact form, or by scheduling a one-on-one consultation with a financial advisor. Additionally, you can join group webinars or events to interact with experts in real-time.

## 13. Is Retire Riches Club suitable for people at any age?

Absolutely! ***Retire Riches Club*** is designed to help individuals of all ages. Whether you are just starting your career, approaching retirement, or already retired, the platform provides tailored advice and resources to suit your unique financial situation.

## 14. How do I track my progress with Retire Riches Club?

Members have access to a personalized dashboard that helps track their financial progress, monitor investment performance, and adjust their strategies as needed. This tool ensures you stay on course to achieve your retirement goals.

## 15. What sets Retire Riches Club apart from other retirement planning services?

***Retire Riches Club*** offers a combination of personalized attention, expert advice, and comprehensive tools tailored to each member's financial goals. Unlike generic platforms,

***Retire Riches Club*** focuses on long-term wealth creation, helping you retire rich and secure a comfortable future.

What's app: 0 9560712121

Email: retirerichesclub@gmail.com

# *Thank You!*

I want to extend my deepest and most heartfelt gratitude to you for taking the time to read this book. Your support means more to me than words can express, and I am truly honoured that you chose to embark on this journey with me. Writing this book has been **passion-driven endeavour**, and knowing that it is now in your hands fills me with immense joy and gratitude.

I sincerely hope that the insights, strategies, and lessons shared within these pages have provided you with knowledge, inspiration, and a renewed sense of confidence in your financial future. Whether you are just beginning your retirement planning journey or refining your approach, my greatest wish is that this book serves as a trusted guide in helping you build the life you envision—one filled with security, independence, and peace of mind.

Your trust and support mean everything to me, and I do not take it for granted. If this book has added even a small amount of value to your life, I would be deeply appreciative of your thoughts and feedback. Your journey toward financial freedom and a fulfilling retirement is one of the most important steps you will ever take, and I am honoured to be a small part of that process.

From the bottom of my heart, thank you for your time, your belief in the ideas shared here, and for allowing me to contribute to your financial well-being. I wish you endless success, prosperity, and a future filled with abundance and joy.

**With immense gratitude and best wishes,**
*Anurag Mishra*

Author & Founder of ***Retire Riches Club***

*Real-Life Stories of Retirees Facing Financial Collapse Due to Lack of Planning*

Many retirees in India find themselves in dire financial situations because they either didn't plan for retirement, underestimated their future expenses, or failed to invest wisely. Here are a few real-life stories that highlight the harsh realities of ignoring financial planning.

### 1. The Pension That Wasn't Enough – The Story of Mr. Sharma

*"I thought my pension would be enough. I was wrong."*

**Mr. Sharma**, a retired government employee from Delhi, spent his entire career believing that his pension and provident fund would be sufficient. When he retired at 60, he had about **₹30 lakh in his PF and a pension of ₹25,000 per month**.

Initially, things seemed fine. But as medical expenses started rising, inflation eroded his purchasing power, and unforeseen home repairs came up, his pension was no longer enough. Worse, his **sons moved abroad** and were unable to provide financial support. Within 10 years, his savings were nearly exhausted, and by 75, he was forced to **sell his ancestral home** and move into a smaller rental.

*☞ Lesson: A pension alone is not enough. Inflation and medical costs can wipe out savings faster than expected.*

## 2. The Businessman Who Lost It All – The Story of Mr. Iyer

*"I earned in crores but never saved. Now, I survive on my daughter's salary."*

**Mr. Iyer** was a successful textile businessman in Mumbai, earning lakhs every month. He lived a lavish lifestyle—frequent international trips, expensive gadgets, and luxury cars. He always thought his business would support him forever.

Then came **the 2008 recession**, which hit his industry hard. Orders declined, debts piled up, and he had no emergency funds or investments to fall back on. By the time he turned 60, he had **no active income, no savings, and heavy loans**. His **daughter had to step in to support him financially**.

☞ *Lesson: High income doesn't guarantee financial security. Without savings and investments, even the richest can fall.*

## 3. The Widow Left with Nothing – The Story of Mrs. Joshi

*"I trusted my husband to handle everything. After he passed, I had nothing."*

**Mrs. Joshi**, a homemaker from Pune, had always depended on her husband to handle finances. He was a responsible man, but he never thought of securing her financially beyond his salary. When he passed away suddenly at 65, she discovered that:

- ➢ He had no life insurance.
- ➢ Their savings were minimal, as he had spent most of it on their children's weddings.
- ➢ He had never invested in assets that would generate passive income.

With no financial knowledge and no income, she had to **depend on relatives for survival**. The emotional and financial stress took a toll on her health.

☞ *Lesson: Financial planning should involve both spouses. Relying solely on one person's knowledge can be disastrous.*

## 4. The EPF That Vanished Too Soon – The Story of Mr. Rao

*"I thought ₹50 lakh was enough for retirement. It wasn't."*

**Mr. Rao**, an IT professional from Bangalore, retired with ₹50 lakh in his EPF account. He believed this amount would last a lifetime. However, within **five years, it was nearly gone** because:

- ➢ He withdrew large amounts for home renovations and family vacations.
- ➢ Inflation and rising healthcare costs ate into his corpus.
- ➢ He made some bad investment choices in unknown schemes, which resulted in losses.

At 70, with no income left, he had to **go back to work as a part-time consultant** to meet his expenses.

☞ *Lesson: A lump sum is not enough—you need a strategy to make your money last.*

## *The Common Mistakes That Led to Their Financial Collapse*

- **Delaying or avoiding investments** – Thinking they had "enough time" and never starting.

- **Relying solely on pensions or savings** – Not accounting for inflation, healthcare, and emergencies.

- **Not planning for life expectancy** – Many outlived their savings.

- **Spending instead of investing** – Using their retirement corpus for weddings, vacations, or unnecessary expenses.

- **Lack of financial education** – Not understanding investments, insurance, or tax-efficient withdrawals.

## How to Avoid Their Fate

✅ **Start early** – Invest in PPF, NPS, mutual funds, and SIPs as early as possible.

✅ **Plan for healthcare** – Get a health insurance policy to avoid medical bankruptcy.

✅ **Diversify investments** – Don't rely only on EPF or pension; build multiple income streams.

✅ **Involve your spouse** – Both partners should understand and participate in financial planning.

✅ **Think long-term** – Your money should last at least **25-30 years post-retirement**.

## Final Thought

These stories are **not just cautionary tales—they are real-life lessons**. Retirement is supposed to be a time of peace and security, not stress and financial struggle. The only way to ensure a comfortable future is to **start planning and investing today**.

*◆ Do you have a retirement plan? If not, now is the time to take action!*

## *Notes: Living a Liability-Free Life – The Key to Stress-Free Retirement*

### Introduction

Financial freedom is not just about earning and investing—it's also about being free from liabilities. A life without unnecessary debt allows you to save, invest, and retire with peace of mind. While loans can help in achieving financial goals, excessive debt can become a burden that affects your long-term security.

In this chapter, we'll explore the **pros and cons of loans**, their impact on retirement, and strategies for living a **liability-free life** with real-life examples.

### Understanding Loans: Good Debt vs. Bad Debt

Not all debt is bad. Some loans can help you build wealth, while others can drain your finances.

### Pros of Loans (Good Debt)

✓ **Home Loans** – Buying a house with a loan can be a wise investment if its value appreciates.

✓ **Education Loans** – Investing in education can enhance earning potential.

✓ **Business Loans** – Borrowing to start or expand a business can create wealth over time.

✓ **Asset-Backed Loans** – Loans used to buy appreciating assets (like real estate) can be beneficial.

### Cons of Loans (Bad Debt)

✗ **Credit Card Debt** – High-interest rates can lead to financial stress.

✘ **Personal Loans for Lifestyle Expenses** – Borrowing for vacations, gadgets, or weddings can erode savings.

✘ **Car Loans** – Vehicles depreciate quickly, making auto loans a poor financial choice unless necessary.

✘ **Multiple EMIs** – Juggling too many loans reduces disposable income and savings potential.

📌 **Tip:** The key is to use loans **strategically** and avoid unnecessary liabilities that don't generate value.

## How Debt Impacts Your Retirement

Carrying liabilities into retirement can be dangerous. Here's why:

### 1. Reduced Savings Potential

Every EMI you pay reduces the money available for investments. If ₹20,000 per month goes to EMIs, that's ₹2.4 lakh per year lost from your retirement savings.

### 2. Higher Financial Stress

Managing debt during retirement with no active income can lead to stress, forcing retirees to **compromise on lifestyle and healthcare.**

### 3. Increased Dependency

Many retirees with outstanding loans end up relying on children for financial support, which can strain family relationships.

### 4. Risk of Asset Liquidation

In extreme cases, retirees may be forced to **sell assets like property or jewellery** to clear debts, affecting financial security.

## Real-Life Examples

### Example 1: The Debt-Free Retiree – Mr. Mehta's Story

Mr. Mehta, a software engineer, **cleared all his home and car loans by age 50**. Instead of taking new loans, he prioritized savings and investments. By 60, he had a **debt-free home, sufficient retirement corpus, and no financial stress**. His disciplined approach allowed him to enjoy a comfortable and worry-free retirement.

📌 **Lesson:** Prepaying loans before retirement ensures financial independence.

### Example 2: The Burdened Retiree – Mr. Sharma's Struggle

Mr. Sharma, a businessman, took multiple loans for luxury cars, vacations, and home renovations. At 60, he still had outstanding liabilities of ₹50 lakh. Since his income stopped after retirement, his EMIs consumed a major portion of his pension, forcing him to sell his second home to clear debts.

📌 **Lesson:** Excessive loans can wipe out retirement savings and force asset liquidation.

### Strategies for Living a Liability-Free Life

✅ **Avoid Unnecessary Loans** – Differentiate between essential and non-essential debt.

✅ **Prepay Loans Early** – Try to clear all debts before retirement.

✅ **Build an Emergency Fund** – Avoid borrowing for sudden expenses.

✅ **Invest Instead of Borrowing** – Use investments for big expenses rather than loans.

☑ **Live Within Means** – Avoid lifestyle inflation that leads to unnecessary debt.

**Conclusion**

A liability-free life ensures that your retirement years are spent in peace, not worrying about EMIs and debts. While some loans can be beneficial, excessive liabilities can **derail financial independence**. The best approach is to **borrow wisely, repay early, and enter retirement completely debt-free.**

◆ *Start planning today for a secure tomorrow!*

**Coming Soon….**

*Financial Independence, Retire Early (FIRE)*

**Introduction to FIRE**

Imagine waking up every morning with the freedom to choose how you spend your day—free from the constraints of a 9-to-5 job. This is the essence of the Financial Independence, Retire Early (FIRE) movement, a lifestyle choice that prioritizes aggressive saving, smart investing, and frugality to achieve early retirement.

FIRE is not just about quitting work; it's about gaining financial control and designing a life that aligns with your passions and values. Whether you dream of traveling the world, spending more time with family, or pursuing passion projects, FIRE provides a roadmap to make it possible.

**The Core Principles of FIRE**

**1. Financial Independence (FI)**

Financial independence means having enough wealth to cover your living expenses indefinitely without relying on traditional employment. This is typically achieved through investments, passive income streams, and low-cost living. The general rule is to accumulate 25 to 30 times your annual expenses, based on the 4 % withdrawal rule, though in the Indian context, a more conservative 3.5% withdrawal rate may be advisable due to inflation and lack of social security.

**2. Retire Early (RE)**

Retiring early doesn't necessarily mean never working again. Many FIRE followers continue to work on passion projects, part-time gigs, or businesses they enjoy. The key difference is that they work because they want to, not because they have to.

**Steps to Achieve FIRE in India**

**1. Maximize Your Savings Rate**

A fundamental aspect of FIRE is saving an exceptionally high percentage of your income—typically 50% to 75%. In India, where salaries vary widely, this requires cutting unnecessary expenses, leveraging tax benefits, and increasing income through career growth or side hustles.

**2. Invest Wisely**

Your savings need to work for you. FIRE enthusiasts in India typically invest in:

- Hybrid funds (e.g., Nifty 50 and Sensex funds) for long-term growth.
- Public Provident Fund (PPF) and Employees' Provident Fund (EPF) for tax-efficient, risk-free returns.
- Real estate for rental income, especially in Tier-2 and Tier-3 cities with growth potential.
- Dividend-paying stocks and Mutual funds.
- Side businesses or alternative investments such as gold and bonds.

**3. Control Expenses and Avoid Lifestyle Inflation**

Many people increase their spending as their income rises. FIRE followers resist this temptation, keeping expenses in check even as they earn more. In India, this means living in affordable housing, avoiding unnecessary loans, and leveraging discounts, cashback offers, and government subsidies.

## 4. Eliminate Debt

High-interest debt is a major obstacle to FIRE. Prioritizing debt repayment—especially credit cards, personal loans, and high-interest EMIs—frees up more money for investing and wealth accumulation.

## 5. Build Passive Income Streams

The goal of FIRE is to replace active income with passive income. Common sources include:

- ➢ Rental properties (especially in emerging cities).
- ➢ Stock dividends and Systematic Withdrawal Plans (SWPs) from Mutual Funds.
- ➢ Business income.
- ➢ Royalties from books, blogs, or other creative work.

### Variations of FIRE in India

FIRE is not a one-size-fits-all approach. There are several variations tailored to different financial goals and lifestyles:

### 1. Lean FIRE

This version requires extremely low living expenses, often below ₹6-12 lakhs per year, by adopting a frugal lifestyle.

### 2. Fat FIRE

For those who want financial independence but don't want to compromise on a higher standard of living, Fat FIRE requires a larger portfolio, usually allowing for annual spending of ₹25 lakhs or more.

### 3. Coast FIRE

Coast FIRE means accumulating enough wealth early in life so that future savings are unnecessary. By letting investments grow, you can eventually retire without additional contributions.

## 4. Barista FIRE

This approach combines early retirement with part-time work for additional income and benefits, such as healthcare and insurance, which are crucial in India due to the lack of universal healthcare.

## Challenges and Considerations in India

While FIRE offers financial freedom, it requires discipline and sacrifice. Some challenges include:

- ➤ **Market Volatility**: The Indian stock market is still developing, and a market downturn could impact early retirement plans.

- ➤ **Healthcare Costs**: Without employer-sponsored insurance, managing healthcare costs is a major consideration. Opting for a robust health insurance policy is crucial.

- ➤ **Family and Social Expectations**: In India, family obligations such as supporting parents, children's education, and social commitments can impact savings goals.

- ➤ **Inflation and Cost of Living**: India's inflation rate tends to be higher than that of Western countries, necessitating a larger corpus for long-term sustainability.

- ➤ **Regulatory Changes**: Changes in tax laws, investment rules, or pension schemes could impact financial plans.

## Conclusion

The FIRE movement in India & all the world is about more than just money—it's about designing a fulfilling life on your terms. While it requires dedication, financial discipline, and strategic planning, the reward is the ability to live life without financial stress. Whether you choose Lean FIRE, Fat FIRE, or somewhere in between, achieving financial independence in India can offer the ultimate freedom: the power to control your time and your future.

To be continued............................................................................
............................................................................

*Retire Riches*

## Thank You

**"Action is the foundational key to all success."**

*Pablo Picasso*

www.ingramcontent.com/pod-product-compliance
Lightning Source LLC
LaVergne TN
LVHW041924070526
838199LV00051BA/2720